TRATTORIA

TRATTORIA

Italian country recipes for home cooks

Maxine Clark *photography by Martin Brigdale*

RYLAND
PETERS
& SMALL

LONDON NEW YORK

First published in the United States in 2004
by Ryland Peters & Small, Inc.
519 Broadway, 5th Floor
New York, NY 10012
www.rylandpeters.com

10 9 8 7 6 5 4 3 2 1

Text © Maxine Clark 2004
Design and photographs
© Ryland Peters & Small 2004

Library of Congress Cataloging-in-
Publication Data

Clark, Maxine.
  Trattoria : Italian country recipes for home
cooks / Maxine Clarke ; photography by
Martin Brigdale.
    p. cm.
  Includes index.
  ISBN 1-84172-709-1
  1. Cookery, Italian. I. Title.
  TX723.C56535 2004
  641.5945--dc22
                  2003028053

Printed and bound in China.

Notes

- All spoon measurements are level unless otherwise stated.
- All herbs are fresh, unless specified otherwise.
- Ingredients in this book are available from larger supermarkets, speciality, and gourmet stores. See page 142 for mail order sources.
- For all recipes requiring dough or batter, liquid measurements are given as a guide. Always add liquid gradually to achieve the desired consistency, rather than adding it all at once. Use your eyes and your sense of touch to achieve the best results. If you don't use the flour specified in a recipe, the result may be affected.
- Eggs are large unless otherwise specified. Uncooked or partially cooked eggs should not be served to the very old, frail, young children, pregnant women, or those with compromised immune systems.
- Ovens should be preheated to the specified temperature. If using a convexion oven. follow the manufacturer's instructions.

Dedication

To Louise and Elisa who have shown me that trattorias still exist.

Author's Acknowledgments

My thanks to Elsa and Alison for commissioning me to do this book, and keeping me on the straight and narrow!
Steve has designed another beautiful book. I hope he didn't put on too much weight when "art directing" at the studio.
My thanks as ever to Martin for his evocative and sensitive photography and Helen for her eclectic and atmospheric propping.
Grateful thanks to Linda for cooking and preparing the dishes to look so edible on the page, with that natural light touch of hers.

Senior Designer Steve Painter
Commissioning Editor
                Elsa Petersen-Schepelern
Production Paul Harding
Art Director Gabriella Le Grazie
Publishing Director Alison Starling

Food Stylist Linda Tubby
Prop Stylist Helen Trent
Indexer Hilary Bird

contents

the family trattoria still exists ...

A good trattoria can be hard to find for the occasional visitor to Italy. As a tourist, you must look hard with eyes wide open, or seek insider information from someone local—there are many to choose from, but few that live up to expectations.

A trattoria is a small restaurant, often family-run, producing homey meals from good, fresh, local ingredients. The menu will be short, change seasonally, but will not be adventurous—for the soul of trattoria food lies in tried and trusted recipes passed down through generations, often evoking memories of meals eaten at home cooked by your mother or grandmother during childhood. You feel safe in a cozy, welcoming trattoria. The bustling family atmosphere, still key to Italian life, and the familiar smells assailing your nostrils will cocoon you like a security blanket.

Successful trattorias can stay in the same family for generations—the job of cooking passing from grandfather or grandmother to daughter or son and so on. Gender does not matter in the kitchen: it's the ability to cook with love that matters. When grandparents become too frail to stand the rigors of a busy kitchen, they fulfil other useful jobs such as prepping vegetables, giving advice (wanted or not!), waiting at tables, manning the cash desk, or taking time to make one dish that remains their personal speciality. After service has finished at lunch or dinner, the family will sit around a table and eat their own meal, discussing family matters and the events of the day. This is not a dreamworld: it still exists.

Locality, good food, and a warm welcome are the traditional hallmarks. Any Italian trattoria will have its regulars, whether at lunch or dinner, and eating alone is not a problem.

Recently I visited a trattoria in Florence with an Australian-Italian friend. When she was a child, her parents used to take her to this place, just off a busy street in the center, but easy to pass by. She was returning 20 years later and was very apprehensive. We went in single file to our table in the long corridor that was the dining room. There was no room for elbows, never mind the coats and scarves we were wearing on a damp October day. The place hadn't changed at all. It was full of working Florentines having lunch. My friend caught the eye of the slightly bent, gruff old man, smartly dressed in black with a snowy apron hanging from ample waist to ankle.

She told him that she recognized him from 20 years earlier, and a brusque but animated conversation ensued, sealed with firm handshakes and a big toothy smile. We asked for what was good that day and weren't disappointed. Everything was typically Tuscan, without frills, and cooked to perfection. The service was fast, the atmosphere warm and congenial, people knew what to expect and got it. So my friend had hoped, and I for one was glad that she hadn't been disappointed. Laughing and contented, we walked out of that place and into the sophistication of Florence.

The family-run trattoria will still be there, if you look.

antipasti

The contrast of the golden crunchy bread crumbs and the soft mussel meat is fantastic. Although this recipe may seem a lot of work, it is well worth it. Mussels are known as *cozze* in Italian, but called *muscoli* in Tuscany.

baked mussels
with crispy bread crumbs

cozze gratinate

3 lb. fresh mussels, cleaned
(see preparation* page 74)

⅔ cup white wine

2 garlic cloves, lightly crushed

3 tablespoons olive oil

1 onion, very finely chopped

1 cup stale but not dried bread crumbs

¼ cup finely chopped fresh flat-leaf parsley

freshly squeezed juice of 1 lemon

sea salt and freshly ground black pepper

*a large baking dish or
4 individual baking dishes*

a baking tray

serves 4 as an appetizer

Put the mussels in a large saucepan, add the wine and garlic, cover tightly with a lid, and cook over high heat for 4–5 minutes until they JUST start to open. Discard any that do not open. Strain through a colander and reserve the juices.

When the mussels have cooled, twist off all the empty shells and arrange the mussels in a single layer in a large baking dish or individual baking dishes set on a baking tray.

Heat the olive oil in a skillet, add the onion, and sauté for 5 minutes until soft. Reduce the heat, add the parsley and bread crumbs, and stir so all the bread crumbs absorb the oil. Cook for a further 5 minutes to brown the crumbs a little.

Sprinkle this mixture over the mussels, trickle over extra olive oil and the lemon juice, and bake in a preheated oven at 425°F for 5 minutes. Reheat the strained liquid in a saucepan, add salt and pepper to taste (take care because the liquid may already be salty), then pour around the mussels before serving.

One of the finest sights in a southern Italian fish market is a whole tuna fish being deftly portioned by men wielding the sharpest of cleavers, singing and shouting to passers-by to come and buy their magnificent catch. You can be sure it is sparkling fresh, and it is perfect for making *carpaccio*—the Italian equivalent of sashimi. Chilling or lightly freezing it makes it firm enough to slice very thinly. As soon as the slices hit plates at room temperature, they become meltingly soft. I have also seen smoked salmon and smoked swordfish served this way in Italy.

fresh tuna carpaccio

carpaccio di tonno

8 oz. piece of sashimi-grade tuna or swordfish or swordfish loin (thin end)

about 1 cup arugula

freshly shaved Parmesan cheese

dressing

freshly squeezed juice of 3 lemons

⅔ cup extra virgin olive oil

1 garlic clove, finely chopped

1 tablespoon salted capers, rinsed and chopped

a pinch of hot red pepper flakes

sea salt and freshly ground black pepper

serves 4

Trim the tuna of any membrane or gristle. Wrap tightly in plastic wrap and freeze for about 1 hour, until just frozen but not rock solid.

Meanwhile, to make the dressing, put the lemon juice, olive oil, garlic, capers, pepper flakes, salt, and pepper in a bowl and whisk until emulsified.

Unwrap the tuna, slice it thinly with a sharp, thin-bladed knife. Arrange so the slices completely cover 4 large plates. Spoon the dressing over the top. Add a tangle of arugula and sprinkle with shaved Parmesan, then serve.

three marinated antipasti

involtini di peperoni
melanzane con salame e carciofi
zucchine alla griglia marinate al limone

involtini di peperoni

2 large red bell peppers

6 oz. fresh mozzarella cheese

8 large fresh basil leaves

1 tablespoon Classic Pesto (page 140)

extra virgin olive oil

sea salt and freshly ground black pepper

melanzane con salame e carciofi

1 medium eggplant, about 8 oz.

⅓ cup olive oil, plus extra for brushing

8 thin slices salami

4 artichokes marinated in oil,
drained and halved

2 tablespoons freshly squeezed lemon juice

1 tablespoon capers, rinsed,
drained, and chopped

sea salt and freshly ground black pepper

zucchine alla griglia marinate al limone

3 medium zucchini

¼ cup olive oil, plus extra for brushing

2 tablespoons freshly squeezed lemon juice

1 tablespoon freshly grated
Parmesan cheese

2 anchovies, rinsed and finely chopped

toothpicks

serves 4

All too often, antipasti can be very dull, but with a little imagination, you can work wonders with the simplest of ingredients. Marinating these morsels first gives them extra savor. The best antipasti are an appealing mix of colors, flavors, and textures, to whet the palate before the meal ahead.

To make the *involtini*, grill or broil the bell peppers until soft and black. Rinse off the charred skin, cut the peppers in quarters lengthwise, cut off the stalks, and scrape out the seeds. Cut the mozzarella into 8 thin slices. Put a slice inside each pepper strip, put a basil leaf on top, and season well with salt and pepper. Roll up from one end and secure with a toothpick. Put the pesto in a bowl and beat in enough olive oil to thin it to pouring consistency. Add the rolls and toss to coat. Cover and let marinate for at least 2 hours.

To prepare the *melanzane*, heat a ridged stove-top grill pan until hot. Cut the eggplant into 8 thin slices, brush lightly with olive oil, and cook for 2–3 minutes on each side. Put a slice of salami on each one, then a halved artichoke at one side. Fold the eggplant in half to cover the artichoke, secure with a toothpick and put in a shallow dish. Put the ⅓ cup olive oil in a bowl, whisk in the lemon juice, capers, salt, and pepper, then spoon over the eggplant. Cover and let marinate as above.

To prepare the *zucchine*, cut them into long, thin slices, brush with olive oil, and cook on the same grill pan for 2–3 minutes on each side. Transfer to a shallow dish. Put the ¼ cup olive oil, lemon juice, Parmesan, and anchovies in a bowl, beat with a fork, then pour over the zucchini. Cover and let marinate as above. Serve all three as mixed antipasti.

Caponata is rather like ratatouille, but much more exotic. There are dozens of variations of this delectable dish from Sicily, and it is a stalwart on the trattoria menu. Its origins are in little coastal bars (*caupone* in Sicilian) frequented by fishermen in the old days. It often contained soaked, dried ship's biscuit to pad it out and satisfy voracious appetites after a long fishing trip. The biscuit has long since disappeared and the dish has become somewhat refined. It improves with age, so make a big batch and keep in the refrigerator or preserve in large jars. It's served as an antipasto, but is delicious with grilled fish or steak. As always in Sicily and in hot weather, serve at room temperature—it tastes much better.

sweet and sour sicilian eggplant stew

caponata

4 medium eggplant, cut into bite-size cubes

¼ cup olive oil

1 onion, chopped

2 celery stalks, sliced

12 very ripe large tomatoes, coarsely chopped, or 28 oz. canned chopped tomatoes

1–2 tablespoons salted capers, rinsed well

½ cup best green olives, pitted

2 tablespoons red wine vinegar

2 teaspoons sugar

vegetable oil, for frying

sea salt

to serve

8 oz. fresh ricotta cheese

toasted chopped almonds

freshly chopped flat-leaf parsley

an electric deep-fryer

serves 6

Put the eggplant in a colander, sprinkle with salt, and let drain for 30 minutes.

Heat the olive oil in a saucepan and add the onion and celery. Cook for 5 minutes until softened but not browned, add the tomatoes, then cook for 15 minutes until pulpy. Add the capers, olives, vinegar, and sugar to the sauce and cook for a further 15 minutes.

Rinse the eggplant cubes and pat them dry with paper towels.

Heat the vegetable oil in a deep-fryer to 375°F, add the eggplant in batches, and fry until deep golden brown. This may take some time, but cook them thoroughly, because undercooked eggplant is unpleasant. Alternatively, toss the cubes in olive oil, spread in a roasting pan and roast at 400°F for about 20 minutes until well browned and tender. Drain well.

Stir the eggplant into the sauce. Taste and adjust the seasoning (this means adding more sugar or vinegar to taste to balance the flavors). Set aside for 30 minutes or overnight to develop the flavors before serving. Serve warm or at room temperature (never refrigerator-cold) in a shallow bowl and top with the ricotta, almonds, and parsley.

During the season, asparagus in all its varieties— from purple-tipped, to green, or white (the beloved one)—is often served with egg in some form, especially in the north. I have eaten this in spring in the lovely town of Asolo. All *trattorie* will have fresh asparagus on the menu at this time, and it is eaten as if it will never appear again. To our taste, asparagus is overcooked in Italy, especially in restaurants, but this is how they serve it, and I must say, the slightly longer cooking does bring out the flavor. The truffle oil is an optional luxury—you could add some chopped tarragon to the cream—but it is wonderful with egg and asparagus.

asparagus
with egg and truffle butter

asparagi al burro d'oro

4 fresh free-range eggs

6 tablespoons unsalted butter, softened

a little truffle oil (optional)

1 lb. fresh asparagus

sea salt and freshly ground black pepper

serves 4

Hard-cook the eggs for about 10 minutes, depending on size. Cool in cold water, then peel. Halve the eggs and remove the yolks. Finely chop the whites and reserve. Mash the yolks with the butter until well blended. Add a drop or two of truffle oil, if using, and season with salt. Cover and keep at room temperature.

Trim the asparagus. Steam for about 12 minutes until tender. Arrange on 4 warm plates, sprinkle with chopped egg white, salt, and pepper, then serve with the golden butter. (The butter can either be spooned on top to melt into the spears or served in little dishes to spread onto each mouthful.)

The combination of sweet, salty Parma ham or a local *prosciutto crudo* and a yielding soft fruit like ripe figs or melon is one of life's little miracles. This is an all-time classic, and none the worse for that. I have been served this with a little trickle of aged balsamic vinegar over the figs, which was amazing. If you find a really aged balsamic on your travels, buy it—never mind the expense. It will be thick, sweet, and syrupy, and heaven to use in tiny amounts. In another tiny trattoria I visited, *la signora* wrapped prosciutto around halved figs, brushed them with olive oil and lightly grilled them over charcoal—heaven. This is quick to assemble, providing you have excellent, thinly sliced ham and perfect, garnet-centered figs.

parma ham with figs
and balsamic dressing

4 large or 8 small fresh ripe figs (preferably purple ones)

1 tablespoon good balsamic vinegar

extra virgin olive oil

12 thin slices of Parma ham or *prosciutto crudo*

6 oz. fresh Parmesan cheese, broken into craggy lumps

to serve

extra virgin olive oil

crushed black pepper

serves 4

Take each fig and stand it upright. Using a sharp knife, make 2 cuts across each fig not quite quartering it, but keeping it intact. Ease the figs open and brush with balsamic vinegar and olive oil.

Arrange 3 slices of Parma ham on each plate with the figs and Parmesan on top. Sprinkle with extra virgin olive oil and plenty of crushed black pepper.

There's nothing quite like these light, fresh, silvery morsels eaten fillet by fillet with a glass of chilled *vino bianco*, overlooking a peacock sea, with a warm salty breeze on your face. If you've never tried a fresh anchovy before, and see them in a market—buy them. They are mild and fresh, and the combination of lemon, parsley, and olive oil is lifted by the zing of scallions. Anchovies like these are found all over coastal areas, but you can make this dish with any small fish such as tiny sardines.

marinated fresh anchovies

acciughe al limone

16 fresh anchovies or small sardines

freshly squeezed juice of 2 lemons

2 fat scallions, thinly sliced

2 tablespoons chopped fresh flat-leaf parsley

extra virgin olive oil

sea salt and freshly ground black pepper

serves 4

To clean the anchovies, cut off the heads and slit open the bellies. Remove the insides (there isn't very much there at all) under running water. Slide your thumb along the backbone to release the flesh along its length. Take hold of the backbone at the head end and lift it out. The fish should now open up like a book. At this stage you can decide whether to cut it into 2 long fillets or leave whole—size will dictate. Pat them dry with paper towels.

Pour the lemon juice through a strainer into a shallow non-reactive dish and add the anchovies in an even layer, skin side up. Cover and let marinate in the refrigerator for 24 hours.

The next day, lift them out of the lemon juice—they will look pale and "cooked." Arrange them on a serving dish. Sprinkle with the scallions, parsley, and a large quantity of olive oil, season with salt and pepper, and serve at room temperature.

primi piatti

Pappa al pomodoro is only as good as its ingredients—great tomatoes, good bread, and wonderful, green (preferably Tuscan) olive oil. This is one of the most comforting soups on earth and of course has its origins in peasant thrift. Leftover bread is never thrown away in Tuscany—there is always a use for it. Here, it thickens a rich tomato soup, which is in turn enriched with Parmesan (a nod to modern tastes, because an aged local pecorino would have been used instead). You see this soup on every menu around Florence, Siena, and Arezzo, but it is hard to find a good one—this is worth making just to see how good it can be. My own addition is the basil oil—in Tuscany you would be given olive oil at the table to pour over the soup yourself.

1½ quarts vegetable, chicken, or meat stock

¼ cup olive oil

1 onion, chopped

2½ lb. very ripe, soft tomatoes, coarsely chopped

10 oz. stale white bread, thinly sliced, crusts removed (or bread crumbs)

3 garlic cloves, crushed

1¼ cups freshly grated Parmesan cheese, plus extra to serve

sea salt and freshly ground black pepper

basil oil

⅓ cup freshly chopped basil

⅔ cup extra virgin olive oil

serves 6

creamy tomato and bread soup with basil oil

pappa al pomodoro con olio verde

Heat the stock slowly in a large saucepan. Meanwhile, heat the oil in a second large saucepan, add the onion and tomatoes, and sauté over gentle heat for about 10 minutes until soft. Push the mixture through a food mill or sieve, and stir into the hot broth. Add the bread and garlic.

Cover and simmer gently for about 45 minutes until thick and creamy, beating from time to time to break up the bread. Take care, because this soup can catch on the bottom.

Meanwhile, to make the basil oil, put the basil and olive oil in a blender and blend until completely smooth—if not, pour through a fine strainer.

To finish, stir the Parmesan into the soup, then add salt and pepper to taste. Ladle into bowls and trickle 2 tablespoons basil oil over each serving. Serve hot, warm, or cold (but never chilled), with more Parmesan separately.

1½ cups dried cannellini beans or other white beans

⅔ cup extra virgin olive oil

1 onion, finely chopped

1 carrot, chopped

1 celery stalk, chopped

2 leeks, finely chopped

4 garlic cloves, finely chopped, plus 1 extra peeled and bruised, for rubbing

1 small white cabbage, finely sliced

1 large potato, chopped

4 medium zucchini, chopped

1¾ cups tomato passata (strained, crushed tomatoes)

2 sprigs of rosemary

2 sprigs of thyme

2 sprigs of sage

1 dried red chile

1 lb. *cavolo nero* (Tuscan black cabbage) or Savoy cabbage, finely sliced

6 thick slices coarse crusty white bread

sea salt and freshly ground black pepper

to serve

extra virgin olive oil

freshly grated Parmesan cheese

serves 8 generously

There's nothing quite like a huge plate of thick, warming *ribollita* on a damp fall evening beside a crackling, scented log fire. Best made in large quantities, this is a great soup for a family get-together and is very filling. *Ribollita* means "reboiled," and is made from whatever vegetables are around, but must contain beans and the delicious Tuscan black winter cabbage, *cavolo nero*. I know I am back in Tuscany when I see it growing in rows in small gardens, looking like mini palm trees. Savoy cabbage makes a good alternative. The basic bean and vegetable soup is made the day before, then reheated and ladled over toasted garlic bread, sprinkled with olive oil, and served with lots of Parmesan cheese.

la ribollita

Put the beans in a bowl, cover with cold water, soak overnight, then drain just before you're ready to use them.

Next day, heat half the olive oil in a large, heavy saucepan and add the onion, carrot, and celery. Cook gently for 10 minutes, stirring frequently. Add the leeks and garlic and cook for 10 minutes. Add the white cabbage, potato, and zucchini, stir well, and cook for 10 minutes, stirring frequently.

Stir in the soaked beans, passata, rosemary, thyme, sage, dried chile, salt, and plenty of black pepper. Cover with about 2 quarts water (the vegetables should be well covered), bring to a boil, then turn down the heat and simmer, covered, for at least 2 hours, until the beans are very soft.

Take out 2–3 large ladles of soup and mash well. Stir back into the soup to thicken it. Stir in the *cavolo nero* or Savoy cabbage and simmer for another 15 minutes.

Remove from the heat, let cool, then refrigerate overnight. The next day, slowly reheat the soup and stir in the remaining olive oil. Toast the bread and rub with garlic. Pile the bread in a tureen or in individual bowls and ladle the soup over the top. Trickle in more olive oil and serve with plenty of freshly grated Parmesan.

Toscanelli are the small beans grown and eaten by Tuscan *mangiafagioli* ("bean eaters"). It is a simple soup to be found in various guises all over central and northern Italy. To give it a sophisticated touch, I sauté sliced garlic, rosemary, and chile in good olive oil, just enough to release their scent, and spoon this over the soup just before serving. The aroma is intoxicating. Like many other rugged soups, it is often served as an entrée ladled over toasted country bread.

tuscan bean soup
with rosemary

zuppa di toscanelli al rosmarino

1½ cups dried white or brown beans
(such as haricot, cranberry, or cannellini)

a pinch of baking soda

cold water, or chicken or vegetable stock
(see method)

a handful of fresh sage leaves,
plus 2 tablespoons chopped fresh sage

4 garlic cloves

1¼ cups olive oil

2 tablespoons chopped fresh rosemary

a large pinch of hot red pepper flakes

sea salt and freshly ground black pepper

coarsely chopped fresh flat-leaf parsley,
to serve

serves 6

Put the beans in a bowl, cover with cold water, add a pinch of baking soda, soak overnight, then drain just before you're ready to use them.

Put the drained beans in a flameproof casserole. Cover with cold water or chicken or vegetable stock to a depth of 2 inches above the beans, and push in the handful of sage. Bring to a boil, cover tightly with a lid, and transfer to a preheated oven at 325°F for about 1 hour or until tender. (The time depends on the freshness of the beans—test after 40 minutes.) Keep them in their cooking liquid.

Meanwhile, finely chop 2 of the garlic cloves, and thinly slice the remainder. Put half the beans, the cooked sage (minus any stalks), and all the liquid into a blender or food processor and blend until smooth. Pour back into the remaining beans in the casserole. If the soup is thicker than you like, add extra water or stock to thin it down.

Heat half the olive oil in a skillet and add the chopped garlic. Sauté gently until soft and golden, then add the chopped sage and cook for 30 seconds. Stir this into the soup and reheat until boiling. Simmer gently for 10 minutes. Add salt and pepper to taste.

Pour into a heated tureen or soup bowls. Heat the remaining olive oil in a small skillet, add the sliced garlic, and sauté carefully until golden (don't let it go too dark or it will be bitter). Stir in the rosemary and pepper flakes. Dip the base of the skillet in cold water to stop the garlic cooking. Spoon the garlic and oil over the soup, then serve sprinkled with chopped fresh parsley.

A typical way to thicken and enrich a broth in many parts of Italy is to add beaten eggs. This is one of the best I have tasted because of the freshness of the greens. Although most of us are limited to spinach, there are many more varieties of *ortaggi* (greens) in Italian markets—beet tops, for example, or even zucchini leaves and tendrils. Just outside Modena, this soup was rustled up for me in minutes, as I had arrived too late for anything else. Served with a basket of bread and some homemade salame afterwards, it was just perfect.

spinach broth
with egg and cheese

minestra di spinaci, uova e parmigiano

1½ lb. fresh spinach

4 tablespoons butter

4 eggs

⅓ cup freshly grated Parmesan

¼ teaspoon freshly grated nutmeg

about 1¾ quarts good chicken stock

sea salt and freshly ground black pepper

serves 6

Remove all the stalks from the spinach, then wash the leaves thoroughly—do not shake dry. Cook the leaves in a large saucepan with the water still clinging. When the leaves have wilted, drain well, then chop finely.

Heat the butter in a medium saucepan, then add the spinach, tossing well to coat with the butter. Remove from the heat and let cool for 5 minutes.

Put the eggs, Parmesan, nutmeg, salt, and pepper in a bowl and beat well. Mix into the spinach. Put the stock in a large saucepan and bring almost to a boil. When almost boiling, beat in the spinach and egg mixture as quickly as you can to avoid separating. Reheat gently without boiling for a couple of minutes and serve immediately.

Picking wild mushrooms is a late-summer-to-fall passion for all Italians, and for me in my native Scotland, with the *porcino* ("little pig" or *Boletus edulis*) being the most prized. In the Chianti hills or in Umbria, you can drive up winding country roads and notice cars tucked into the bushes along the way, but hardly ever see a person—everyone is deep in the undergrowth searching for mushrooms. Wild mushrooms have a strong, earthy taste—almost meaty—and are piled high on a display table in a trattoria I love near Civitella in Tuscany. The combination of creamy chickpeas and earthy mushrooms is unusual and absolutely captivating—very "Umbro-Toscano."

cream of chickpea soup
with wild mushrooms

crema di ceci ai porcini

4 tablespoons butter

2 oz. *cubetti di pancetta*
(cubes of dry-cure smoked bacon)

6 oz. fresh wild mushrooms or dark portobello mushrooms, plus 1 oz. dried porcini mushrooms, soaked in warm water for 20 minutes to soften

2 shallots, finely chopped

2 garlic cloves, coarsely chopped

freshly squeezed juice of 1 lemon

14 oz. canned chickpeas, drained

1½ quarts chicken or vegetable stock

⅔ cup heavy cream

3 tablespoons freshly chopped flat-leaf parsley

sea salt and freshly ground black pepper

serves 6

Put the butter in a large saucepan, melt gently, then add the pancetta, and sauté slowly until golden.

Put the mushrooms, shallots, and garlic in a food processor and chop finely, using the pulse button. Add the mushroom mixture to the pancetta and cook, stirring over medium to high heat, for about 15 minutes, until all the juices have evaporated and the mixture becomes a thick paste. Stir in the lemon juice and chickpeas. Beat in the stock and bring to a boil. Cover and simmer for 25 minutes.

Transfer the soup, in batches if necessary, to a blender or food processor and blend until smooth. Return the soup to the rinsed-out pan and stir in the cream. Add salt and pepper to taste, then stir in the parsley and reheat without boiling, or the soup may separate.

A lovely soup to serve in the summer when fresh peas and mint are plentiful. Vialone nano is the favorite risotto rice in the Veneto region. It is a semi-fino round-grain rice, best for soups and risotti, but arborio (a superfino used mainly for risotti) will do very nicely. This dish has very ancient roots, and was flavored with fennel seeds at one time. Parsley is the usual addition now, but I prefer mint in the summer.

venetian pea and rice soup
with mint

risi e bisi con la menta

5 cups chicken, beef, or vegetable broth

2 tablespoons olive oil

4 tablespoons butter

2 oz. pancetta, finely chopped

1 large scallion (*cipolloto*), or the white parts of 4 scallions, finely chopped

1 cup risotto rice, preferably vialone nano

2½ lb. fresh peas in the pod, shelled, or 1 lb. frozen peas

3 tablespoons freshly chopped mint

freshly grated Parmesan cheese

sea salt and freshly ground black pepper

serves 4

Put the stock in a large saucepan and bring it slowly to a boil while you prepare the *soffrito* (sautéed sauce).

Heat the olive oil and 2 tablespoons of the butter in a large saucepan and, when melted, add the pancetta and scallion. Cook for about 5 minutes until softened but not browned.

Pour in the rice, stir for a few minutes to toast it, then add all the boiling stock. Simmer for 10 minutes, stirring from time to time, then add the peas, cook for 5–7 minutes. Stir in the remaining butter, mint, and Parmesan. Add salt and pepper to taste and serve immediately. The rice grains should not be too mushy, and the soup should be thick, but not stodgy.

Italy produces the most wonderful, comforting soups and this one from Campania combines two of the great stand-bys—beans and pasta. This is real tratt stuff, and brings a smile of nostalgia to the face of any homesick Italian. I think it's because they remember *nonna*'s version more than one from a trattoria!

pasta and bean soup

pasta e fagioli

1¼ cups dried cannellini, haricot beans, or other white beans

a pinch of baking soda

¼ cup olive oil, plus extra to serve

2 garlic cloves, crushed

1¾ quarts chicken stock or water

1 cup short pasta shapes, such as maccheroni or tubetti

4 tomatoes, peeled, seeded, and coarsely chopped

¼ cup freshly chopped flat-leaf parsley

sea salt and freshly ground black pepper

serves 6

Put the beans in a bowl, cover with cold water, add a pinch of baking soda, soak overnight, then drain just before you're ready to use them.

The next day, put the drained beans in a large saucepan. Add the olive oil, garlic, and stock or water. Bring to to a boil, reduce the heat, and simmer, partially covered with a lid, for 1–2 hours or until the beans are tender.

Working in batches if necessary, blend the beans with the cooking liquid using a blender or food processor. Return the bean purée to the rinsed-out pan, adding extra water or stock as necessary. Add the pasta and simmer gently for 15 minutes until tender. (Add a little extra water or stock if the soup is looking too thick.) Stir in the tomatoes and parsley and season well with salt and pepper. Serve with an extra trickle of olive oil.

I have eaten many variations of this dish in Sicily. It is very rich, but this is balanced by grated *ricotta salata*—ewe's milk ricotta cheese, salted and aged. It is very dry and concentrated, but sharp and salty. The nearest thing I can find to it outside the area is aged pecorino or even feta cheese. Although a very ancient dish, it has been named *"alla Norma"* by the people of Catania in homage to the composer Vincenzo Bellini, after one of his operas.

spaghetti with eggplant and tomato sauce

pasta alla norma

3 medium eggplant
(round violet ones if possible)

1 lb. very ripe red tomatoes (add
2 tablespoons of tomato paste if
not red enough)

3 tablespoons olive oil

3 garlic cloves, chopped

12 oz. spaghetti or spaghettini

3 tablespoons chopped fresh basil

3–4 tablespoons freshly grated *ricotta salata*, aged pecorino, or Parmesan cheese, plus extra to serve

sea salt and freshly ground black pepper

vegetable oil, for cooking

serves 4

Cut the eggplant into small dice and put in a colander. Sprinkle with salt and put the colander on a plate. Set aside to drain for 30 minutes.

Meanwhile, dip the tomatoes in boiling water for 10 seconds, then drop into cold water. Slip off the skins, cut in half, and squeeze out and discard the seeds. Chop the flesh coarsely.

Heat the olive oil in a skillet, add the garlic, cook for 2–3 minutes until golden, then add the tomatoes. Cook for about 15 minutes until the tomatoes begin to disintegrate.

Bring a large saucepan of salted water to a boil, add the spaghetti, and cook according to the package instructions, about 8 minutes.

Meanwhile, rinse the eggplant, drain, and pat dry. Heat about 1 inch vegetable oil in a skillet, add the cubes of eggplant, and sauté until deep golden brown. Remove and drain on paper towels. Stir into the tomato sauce.

Drain the pasta, reserving 2 tablespoons of the cooking water in the pan and returning the pasta to the hot pan. Stir in the sauce, basil, and grated cheese and serve immediately with more cheese on the side.

Long pasta is the choice for seafood dishes around coastal Italy—spaghetti and spaghettini in the south. This one is another simple dish made with local ingredients—nothing sophisticated, but so good. When buying mussels, make sure that when you tap each one sharply against the work surface it closes—if not, it is dead and should be thrown away. This dish is equally good made with small clams, such as cherrystones.

spaghetti with mussels, tomatoes, and parsley

spaghetti con le cozze

2 lb. live mussels or small clams

½ cup olive oil

1¼ cups dry white wine

16 oz. spaghetti or spaghettini

2 garlic cloves, peeled and crushed

14 oz. canned chopped tomatoes

2 tablespoons freshly chopped flat-leaf parsley

sea salt and freshly ground black pepper

serves 4

Put the mussels in a bowl of cold water and rinse several times to remove any grit or sand. Pull off the beards and scrub well, discarding any that are not firmly closed. Drain.

Heat the oil and wine in a saucepan and add the mussels. Stir over high heat until the mussels open. Remove and discard any that don't open.

Lift out the cooked mussels with a slotted spoon and put them in a bowl. Reserve the liquid. Cook the spaghetti in plenty of boiling water according to the package instructions, about 8 minutes.

Meanwhile, add the garlic to the mussel liquid in the pan. Boil fast to concentrate the flavor. Stir in the tomatoes, return to a boil, and boil fast for 3–4 minutes until reduced. Stir in the mussels and half the parsley and heat through. Taste and season well with salt and pepper.

Drain the pasta, reserving 2 tablespoons of the cooking water in the pan. Return the pasta to the hot pan and stir in the sauce. Sprinkle with the remaining parsley and serve.

It's surprising how popular potato-filled pasta is—I had never imagined it until a friend took me to a little restaurant where her mother did the cooking. This is the ultimate comfort food, with a hidden cube of melting mozzarella flowing out of the middle. You could add all sorts of things to the potatoes—such as chopped capers or olives, but I prefer it as it is. If the herb sauce doesn't appeal, serve the ravioli in meat or chicken broth, or with a thin meat sauce, such as the *ragù* on page 48.

ravioli pillows
with potato and mozzarella

guanciali di patate e mozzarella

4-egg recipe *Pasta all'Uovo* (page 137)

freshly grated Parmesan cheese, to serve

potato filling

1 lb. medium potatoes, unpeeled

3 tablespoons butter, cubed

½ cup freshly grated Parmesan cheese

¼ teaspoon freshly grated nutmeg

1 egg, plus 1 egg yolk, beaten

2 tablespoons chopped fresh parsley

8 oz. fresh mozzarella cheese, cut into ½-inch cubes to give about 20

sea salt and freshly ground black pepper

herb sauce

1 stick unsalted butter

¼ cup mixed chopped fresh rosemary, thyme, and parsley

sea salt and freshly ground black pepper

a pastry bag fitted with ½-inch plain nozzle

a pasta machine (optional)

a pastry brush

a serrated ravioli cutter or knife

serves 4: makes about 20

To make the filling, put the whole potatoes in a saucepan of cold water and bring to a boil. Simmer for about 30 minutes or until they are completely tender when pierced to the center with a skewer. Drain, then, holding them in a clean dish towel, peel off the skin. Press through a potato ricer or sieve.

Mix the potatoes in a bowl with the butter, grated Parmesan, and nutmeg. Beat in the eggs and parsley and season with salt and pepper. Fill the pastry bag with the mixture.

Cut the rested pasta dough into 4 and roll each into a thin sheet. If you are using a pasta machine, roll to the second last setting. Put a piece of pasta on a lightly floured work surface, keeping the other pieces covered with plastic wrap. Pipe small lengths of potato about 1¾ inches long in even rows, spacing them at 1¾ inch intervals across one piece of the dough. Press a cube of mozzarella in the middle of each strip of potato. Using a pastry brush, brush water along the spaces between the mounds of filling, being careful not to wet the work surface or the dough might stick. Using a rolling pin, lift a second sheet of pasta over the dough covered with filling. Press down firmly between the mounds of filling, pushing out any trapped air. Cut into pillow-shaped rectangles with the ravioli cutter or a sharp knife. Transfer to a lightly floured dish towel. Repeat with the remaining filling, mozzarella, and pasta.

To make the sauce, melt the butter in a saucepan with the herbs and season well with salt and pepper. Bring a large saucepan of salted water to a boil. Add the ravioli and cook for 3 minutes until puffy. Drain well and toss with the herb sauce. Serve with freshly grated Parmesan.

I was so intrigued when I saw this on the menu of a family-run trattoria specializing in all sorts of game and mushroom dishes, in the mountains around Aosta, that I had to have them. A dish of perfectly formed, spinach pasta, "William Tell" hats appeared on my plate. They were filled with herb-scented *capriolo* (roebuck), and were dressed simply with olive oil. They were divine, and this is my re-creation using the more accessible cooked beef and pork.

little alpine caps

cappelletti degli alpini

1 recipe *Pasta all'Uovo,* Spinach Pasta variation (page 137), made with 1¼ cups frozen spinach, 2 eggs, and 2 cups flour (more if too wet)

filling

3 oz. cooked roast beef, coarsely chopped

6 oz. cooked roast pork, coarsely chopped

3 tablespoons freshly grated Parmesan cheese

1 tablespoon chopped fresh thyme

2 juniper berries, crushed

freshly grated nutmeg

2 tablespoons fresh bread crumbs

1 extra-large egg

sea salt and freshly ground black pepper

to serve

1¾ cups hot beef broth

extra virgin olive oil

freshly grated Parmesan cheese

a pasta machine

a pastry brush

serves 4

To make the filling, put the beef and pork in a food processor with the Parmesan, thyme, juniper, nutmeg, bread crumbs, egg, salt, and pepper and pulse until finely chopped. Cover and set aside while you roll out the pasta.

Cut the rested pasta dough in half and roll each into a thin sheet. If you are using a pasta machine, roll to the second last setting. Cut the rolled-out pasta into at least twenty 4-inch squares and dust with a little flour.

Take 1 square and cover the rest with plastic wrap. Put a small teaspoon of filling in the middle of the square. Dampen the edges with a wet pastry brush and fold a corner over the filling to meet the opposite corner to form a triangle. Press the edges together to seal, excluding any air. With the long edge towards you, bring the 2 points at either end of the edge together and overlap very slightly. Press together to seal. That's basically the shape—you can turn up a brim if you like. Set each one on a lightly floured dish towel. Repeat with the remaining filling and pasta.

Bring a large saucepan of salted water to a boil. Add the *cappelletti* and cook for 3 minutes until puffy. Drain well, then carefully arrange in 4 warm pasta plates, pour over the hot broth, and serve with olive oil and Parmesan.

The classic version of this dish is pasta layered with meat sauce and creamy *salsa besciamella*. It is very easy to assemble. Make the *ragù* the day before, and the *besciamella* on the day. If you use fresh pasta, it doesn't need precooking, and is layered up as it is. Just make sure the meat sauce is quite liquid. This will be absorbed into the pasta as it cooks. You could vary the recipe by using grated mozzarella cheese instead of the *besciamella,* or by mixing ricotta cheese, spinach, chopped sun-dried tomatoes, Parmesan, and herbs together instead of the meat sauce. Traditional *ragù* contains chicken livers to add richness, but you can leave them out and replace with an additional quantity of ground beef or pork.

lasagne al forno

about 12 sheets dried or fresh *lasagne verdi,* made from Spinach Pasta (page 138) rolled out to the second last setting on the pasta machine

double recipe *Besciamella* (page 139)

about ½ cup freshly grated Parmesan cheese

ragù

3 oz. pancetta or dry-cure smoked bacon in a piece

4 oz. chicken livers

4 tablespoons butter

1 medium onion, finely chopped

1 medium carrot, chopped

1 celery stalk, trimmed and finely chopped

8 oz. lean ground beef

2 tablespoons tomato paste

¼ cup dry white wine

¾ cup beef stock or water

freshly grated nutmeg

sea salt and freshly ground black pepper

a deep baking dish, 10 x 8 inches, buttered

serves 4–6

To make the *ragù*, cut the pancetta into small cubes. Trim the chicken livers, removing any fat or gristle. Cut off any discolored bits, which will be bitter if left on. Coarsely chop the livers.

Melt the butter in a saucepan, add the pancetta, and cook for 2–3 minutes until browning. Add the onion, carrot, and celery and brown these too. Stir in the ground beef and brown until just changing color, but not hardening— break it up with a wooden spoon. Stir in the chicken livers and cook for 2–3 minutes. Add the tomato paste, mix well, and pour in the wine and stock. Season well with nutmeg, salt, and pepper. Bring to a boil, cover, and simmer very gently for as long as you can—2 hours if possible.

Cook the sheets of dried lasagne in plenty of boiling water in batches according to the package instructions. Lift out with a slotted spoon and drain on a clean dish towel. Fresh pasta will not need cooking.

Spoon one-third of the meat sauce into a buttered baking dish. Cover with 4 sheets of lasagne and spread with one-third of the *besciamella*. Repeat twice more, finishing with a layer of *besciamella* covering the whole top. Sprinkle with Parmesan cheese. Bake in a preheated oven at 350°F for about 45 minutes until brown and bubbling. Let stand for 10 minutes to settle and firm up before serving.

This is a real winter-warmer from the north of Italy where polenta is the staple carbohydrate. I have been to a polenta night where the steaming soft cornmeal was poured straight onto a huge wooden board set in the middle of the table. The sauce was poured into a large hollow in the center of the polenta and everyone gathered round to help themselves directly from the pile—no plates necessary. This is still done in some mountain trattorias.

soft polenta with sausage ragù

polenta con ragù di salsiccia

2 teaspoons salt

2 cups instant polenta

freshly grated Parmesan cheese, to serve

sausage ragù

1 lb. fresh Italian pork sausages

2 tablespoons olive oil

1 medium onion, finely chopped

2 cups tomato passata
(strained crushed tomatoes)

⅔ cup dry red wine

6 sun-dried tomatoes in oil,
drained and sliced

sea salt and freshly ground black pepper

serves 4

To make the *ragù*, squeeze the sausage meat out of the skins into a bowl and break up the meat. Heat the oil in a medium saucepan and add the onion. Cook for 5 minutes until soft and golden. Stir in the sausage meat, browning it all over and breaking up the lumps with a wooden spoon. Pour in the passata and the wine. Bring to a boil. Add the sun-dried tomatoes. Simmer for 30 minutes or until well reduced, stirring occasionally. Add salt and pepper to taste.

Meanwhile, bring 5½ cups water to a boil with 2 teaspoons salt. Sprinkle in the polenta, stirring or whisking to prevent lumps forming.

Simmer for 5–10 minutes, stirring constantly, until thickened like soft mashed potato. Quickly spoon the polenta into 4 large, warm soup plates and make a hollow in the center of each. Top with the sausage ragù and serve with grated Parmesan cheese.

Say "*alla Valdostana*," and every Italian will know that there's Fontina cheese in the dish. This is one of the oldest cheeses made in the Valle d'Aosta—it is rich and nutty, and melts very easily. It is also the basis of a type of fondue called *fonduta*. This polenta dish is typical fare in some of the little family restaurants you come across off the trail when skiing in the mountains. Sometimes it comes with a wild mushroom or venison sauce. Just the stuff to keep the cold out and set you on your way.

baked polenta
with fontina and pancetta

polenta pasticciata alla valdostana

2 cups instant polenta (or real polenta flour)

12 oz. Fontina, raclette, or a mixture of grated mozzarella and Cheddar cheese

1 cup freshly grated Parmesan cheese

6 oz. thinly sliced smoked pancetta

sea salt and freshly ground black pepper

*a shallow ovenproof baking dish,
10 x 8 inches, buttered*

serves 6

If using instant polenta, cook according to the package instructions, then turn out into a mound on a wooden board and let cool and set.

To make real polenta, bring 1 quart salted water to a boil, then slowly sprinkle in the polenta flour through your fingers, whisking all the time to stop lumps forming. Cook, stirring with a wooden spoon, for 45 minutes on low heat and then turn out into a mound on a wooden board and let cool and set as before.

Meanwhile, slice the Fontina thinly or grate it. Cut the polenta into slices about ½-inch thick. Arrange a layer of polenta in the ovenproof dish. Top with half the Fontina and half the Parmesan. Add another layer of polenta, then cover with the remaining Fontina and the remaining Parmesan. Finally, add a layer of pancetta.

Bake in a preheated oven at 350°F for 40 minutes until brown and bubbling and the pancetta crisping on top.

Remove from the oven and serve.

Risotto made with red wine is a miracle of flavor combinations. The sweetness from the mushrooms and cheese and the smoky saltiness from the pancetta make this unforgettable. The important thing to remember is to reduce the wine completely to boil off the alcohol and reduce the acidity. This is a risotto to make in the fall or winter, when you need big, comforting flavors. Don't let the risotto overcook and become stodgy.

risotto with red wine, mushrooms, and pancetta

risotto al chianti, funghi e pancetta

¼ cup olive oil
or 5 tablespoons unsalted butter

3 oz. pancetta, finely chopped

1 red onion, finely chopped

8 oz. cremini or porcini mushrooms,
finely chopped

2½ cups Italian risotto rice, such as arborio

1 cup good Chianti wine

about 1½ quarts good-quality light chicken
or meat stock, well heated

1 cup freshly grated Parmesan cheese

2 tablespoons chopped fresh
flat leaf parsley

sea salt and freshly ground black pepper

1 porcini mushroom. sliced and pan-fried in
olive oil until golden, to serve (optional)

serves 6

Heat half the oil or butter in a large saucepan and add the pancetta, cook until the fat begins to run, then add the onion and chopped mushrooms. Cook gently for 5 minutes until softened and translucent.

Stir in the rice and cook for 1–2 minutes until the rice smells toasty and looks opaque. Add the Chianti wine and boil hard until the liquid disappears.

Add a ladle of hot stock and simmer, stirring until absorbed. Continue adding the stock ladle by ladle until only 2 ladles of stock are left. The rice should be tender but still have some bite to it (this should take 15–18 minutes). As soon as the rice is tender, stir in the remaining olive oil and all the Parmesan. Taste and season well with salt and pepper.

Finally, stir in the remaining stock and let stand with the lid on for 5 minutes. Transfer to a large, warmed bowl and sprinkle with parsley. Top with the fried porcini, if using, and serve immediately.

Central and northern Italy are the places to go for good risotto—I've never eaten a good one in the south. Seafood risotto should be creamy and slightly soupy—*all'onda*, meaning "like a wave." The best seafood *risotti* come from the Venice area, where seafood is abundant in the lagoon. Saffron gives a wonderful warm color and musky flavor. Generally, you will never be offered Parmesan with a fish risotto (except perhaps squid ink risotto)—it is frowned upon, so don't ask!

seafood and saffron risotto

risotto ai frutti di mare

1 teaspoon saffron threads

1½ quarts light fish stock

1¼ cups dry white wine

12 oz. uncooked shrimp tails, unpeeled

6 baby squid, cleaned and cut into rings

6 fresh scallops, halved horizontally if large

1 lb. fresh mussels, cleaned

8 oz. fresh cherrystone clams, rinsed

3 tablespoons olive oil

1 onion, finely chopped

2½ cups Italian risotto rice (arborio or vialone nano)

sea salt and freshly ground black pepper

3 tablespoons chopped fresh flat-leaf parsley, to serve

serves 6

Put the saffron in a small bowl and cover with boiling water. Set aside to infuse while you cook the fish.

Pour the stock and wine into a saucepan and heat to simmering point. Add the shrimp and cook for 2 minutes. Add the squid and scallops and cook for a further 2 minutes. Remove them with a slotted spoon and set aside.

Put the mussels and clams into the stock and bring to a boil. Cover and cook for 3–5 minutes or until all the shells have opened. Remove with a slotted spoon and set aside. Keep the stock hot.

Heat the oil in a large saucepan and add the onion. Cook gently for 5 minutes until softened and translucent. Stir in the rice and cook for 1–2 minutes until the rice smells toasty and looks opaque. Add the saffron water and a ladle of stock and simmer, stirring until absorbed. Continue adding the stock, ladle by ladle, until all but 2 ladles of stock remain, and the rice is tender but still has some bite to it. (This should take about 18 minutes.) Taste and season well with salt and pepper.

Finally, stir in the remaining stock and seafood and let stand with the lid on for 5 minutes. Transfer to a large warmed bowl and sprinkle with parsley. Serve immediately.

Soft and golden, these gnocchi are a staple in the Lazio area around Rome. I have added herbs and mustard to the basic mix and like to serve them with roasted rabbit or lamb. Normally they are served with a simple tomato sauce and are a great favorite with children. Did you know that semolina is hard wheat (durum), ground slightly coarser than flour? It is not a special grain on its own.

roman gnocchi
with herbs and semolina

gnocchi alla romana con le erbe

1 quart milk

1⅔ cups semolina

1¾ cups freshly grated Parmesan cheese

1 stick butter

2 egg yolks

1 tablespoon Dijon mustard

2 tablespoons freshly chopped sage

3 tablespoons freshly chopped fresh flat-leaf parsley

sea salt and freshly ground black pepper

a baking sheet lined with plastic wrap

a 2-inch cookie cutter

an ovenproof dish, 10 x 8 inches, well buttered

serves 4–6

Pour the milk into a saucepan and whisk in the semolina. Bring slowly to a boil, stirring all the time until it really thickens—about 10 minutes (it should be quite thick, like choux paste). Beat in half the Parmesan, half the butter, the egg yolks, mustard, sage, and parsley. Add salt and pepper to taste.

Spread the mixture onto the lined baking sheet to a depth of ½ inch. Let cool and set, about 2 hours.

When set, cut into triangles or circles with the cookie cutter. Spread the chopped trimmings in the bottom of the ovenproof dish. Dot with some of the remaining butter and sprinkle with a little Parmesan. Arrange the gnocchi shapes in a single layer over the trimmings. Dot with the remaining butter and Parmesan. Bake in a preheated oven at 400°F for 20–25 minutes until golden and crusty. Let stand for 5 minutes before serving.

Classic potato gnocchi originate in northern Italy, where they are a staple food. They are served just with melted butter and Parmesan, or maybe a tomato sauce, but they are delicious with pesto made from peppery arugula and sweet, creamy walnuts. They must be made with a good floury-textured potato to give them the correct lightness: they should never be like bullets, but puffy pillows of potato. It takes a little practice to make gnocchi really light, as overworking makes them tough. Some expert gnocchi makers use no flour at all—but don't try this at home.

gnocchi
with arugula pesto

gnocchi di patate con pesto di rucola e noci

2½ lb. baking potatoes, unpeeled

1 teaspoon salt

4 tablespoons butter, melted

1 small egg, beaten

1½–1¾ cups all-purpose flour

extra Parmesan cheese, cut into shavings, to serve

arugula pesto

1 cup arugula

2–3 garlic cloves

finely grated zest of 1 unwaxed lemon

½ cup shelled walnuts

¾ cup good olive oil, plus extra to cover

½ cup finely grated Parmesan cheese

sea salt and freshly ground black pepper

serves 4

To make the gnocchi, cook the unpeeled potatoes in boiling water for 20–30 minutes until very tender; drain well.

Meanwhile, to make the pesto, put the arugula, garlic, lemon zest, walnuts, olive oil, Parmesan, salt, and pepper in a food processor and blend until it is the texture you want. Scrape out into a jar, level the surface, and pour in enough olive oil to cover.

Halve the potatoes and press through a potato ricer, or peel and press through a sieve into a bowl. While they are still warm, add the 1 teaspoon salt, the butter, beaten egg, and half the flour. Mix lightly, then transfer to a floured board. Gradually knead in enough of the remaining flour to yield a smooth, soft, slightly sticky dough. Roll the dough into thick sausages, 1 inch diameter. Cut into 1-inch pieces and shape into corks or pull each one down over the back of a fork to produce the traditional ridged outside and the concave inside. Put them on a lightly floured dish towel.

Bring a large saucepan of salted water to a boil. Cook the gnocchi in batches. Drop them into the boiling water and cook for 2–3 minutes or until they float to the surface. Remove with a slotted spoon immediately they rise and keep hot while you cook the remainder. Toss with the pesto and serve immediately, topped with shaved Parmesan.

Note The pesto can be stored in a jar, covered with a layer of oil, for up to 2 weeks in the refrigerator.

I will never forget this tart. I ate it right down in the toe of Italy on my way to Sicily. The husband of the family had been a chef in the north and had decided to return home and regain his sanity. The tart was turned out before us on the little table—the tomatoes could not have been more red nor the basil more green. Nothing could have been so simple—tomatoes simply bursting with flavor, garlic softly singing, and layers of crisp crust melting in every mouthful.

tomato upside-down tart
with basil

sfogliatelle ai pomodori semi-secchi e basilico

8–10 large ripe plum tomatoes (size depending on what will fit the pan)

2 garlic cloves, finely chopped

1 tablespoon dried oregano

¼ cup extra virgin olive oil, plus extra to serve

8 oz. puff pastry dough

sea salt and freshly ground black pepper

a good handful of basil leaves, to serve

a shallow tart pan or sauté pan, 9 inches diameter

serves 4

Cut the tomatoes in half around the middle. Arrange cut side up in the shallow tart pan so that they fit tightly together. Mix the garlic and oregano with the olive oil, salt, and pepper. Spoon or brush the mixture over the cut tomatoes.

Bake in a preheated oven at 325°F for about 2 hours, checking from time to time. They should be slightly shrunk and still brilliantly red. If too dark, they will be bitter. Let cool in the pan (if the pan is very burned, wash it out, brush it with oil, and return the tomatoes). Increase the oven temperature to 400°F.

Roll out the dough to a circle slightly bigger than the pan. Using the rolling pin to help you, lift up the dough and unroll it over the pan, letting the edges drape over the sides. Lightly press the dough down over the tomatoes, but do not trim the edges yet. Bake for 20 minutes until golden.

Let settle for 5 minutes, then trim off the overhanging edges and invert onto a plate. Sprinkle with olive oil and basil leaves and serve.

The recipe for my basic pizza dough was given to me by a gravel-voiced *pizzaiolo* in Sicily. He insists that using a touch of lemon juice in the dough (made with special finely ground semolina flour for making bread, pasta and pizzas) makes it light and crisp, and I have to agree. Adapt this recipe to ordinary all-purpose flour and it works very well, but the crust is not as golden. A Neapolitan dough is made with only Italian "00" flour and no added oil or fat. Whatever the dough, this is a very patriotic pizza—the colors representing the Italian national flag.

pizza alla margherita

1⅗ cups fine Italian semolina flour (*farina di semola*)

½ cake compressed fresh yeast

1 tablespoon lemon juice

1 tablespoon olive oil

a pinch of salt

about 1¼ cups warm water

pizza topping

1 recipe *Salsa Pizzaiola* (page 139)

8 oz. fresh mozzarella cheese, thinly sliced

a good handful of fresh basil leaves

extra olive oil, for trickling

sea salt and freshly ground black pepper

a *"testa"* or terra cotta bakestone or 2 large heavy baking sheets

baking sheets lined with non-stick baking parchment

a baker's peel (optional)

makes 2 thin-crust pizzas, 8–10 inches diameter

Put the bakestone or baking sheets in the oven and preheat to 425°F.

To make the dough, put the semolina flour in a bowl, crumble the fresh yeast into the flour, add the lemon juice, olive oil, and a generous pinch of salt, then add enough of the warm water to form a very soft dough. Transfer to a floured surface and knead for 10 minutes or until smooth and elastic. Put the dough in a clean, oiled bowl (or an oiled plastic bag), cover, and let rise until doubled in size (about 1 hour).

Cut the dough in half and knead each half into a round. Pat or roll the rounds into 10-inch circles, keeping the bases well floured. Transfer the pizzas onto baking sheets lined with nonstick parchment paper. Spread each one lightly with *salsa pizzaiola,* cover with sliced mozzarella, and season with salt and pepper. Let rise in a warm place for 10 minutes, then open the oven door, and slide paper and pizza onto the hot bakestone or baking sheets. If you are brave, try to shoot them into the oven so that they leave the paper behind—this takes practice. Alternatively, use a baker's peel.

Bake for 18–20 minutes, until the crust is golden and the cheese melted but still white. Remove from the oven, sprinkle with basil leaves and olive oil, then eat immediately.

Note In Sicily, we make this with Italian *farina di semola*. It is very finely ground and needs no extra flour. You can grind ordinary semolina into fine flour by working it in a blender for about 2 minutes.

In general, Italians like to stick to the classics when it comes to pizza, but as you can see below, pizza toppings are limitless. I have taken inspiration from a dish I had in Verona, and applied it to a pizza—well, it's just bread and cheese after all, isn't it?

potato pizza

pizza con radicchio, patate e fontina

½ oz. compressed fresh yeast
or 1 tablespoon active dry yeast

a pinch of sugar

1 cup warm water

2⅓ cups all-purpose flour
plus extra, for dusting

1 tablespoon olive oil

a pinch of salt

potato topping

1 medium potato, peeled and
sliced very thinly

6 oz. Fontina, Taleggio, or mozzarella
cheese

1 large head of radicchio, cut into about
8 wedges, brushed with olive oil and
grilled or broiled for 5 minutes

1 tablespoon chopped fresh thyme

sea salt and freshly ground black pepper

extra olive oil, for trickling

a baking pan, about 11 x 13 inches

serves 2–4, depending on appetite

To make the dough, put the fresh yeast and sugar in a medium bowl and beat until creamy. Whisk in the warm water and leave for 10 minutes until frothy. For other yeasts, use according to the package instructions.

Sift the flour into a large bowl and make a hollow in the center. Pour in the yeast mixture, olive oil, and a good pinch of salt. Mix with a round-bladed knife, then your hands, until the dough comes together. Transfer to a floured surface, wash and dry your hands, and knead for 10 minutes until smooth and elastic. The dough should be quite soft, but if too soft to handle, add more flour, 1 tablespoon at a time. Put the dough in a clean, oiled bowl, cover with a damp dish towel or plastic wrap, and let rise until doubled in size—about 1 hour.

When risen, punch down the dough with your fists, then roll out or pat into a rectangle that will fit in the baking pan, pushing it up the sides a little. Cover the top with a thin layer of sliced potato, then half the cheese, the wedges of radicchio, then the remaining cheese. Season with salt and pepper, and sprinkle with thyme.

Trickle oil over the top and let rise in a warm place for 10 minutes. Bake in a preheated oven at 425°F for 15–20 minutes or until golden and bubbling.

Italians are very thrifty, and a really delicious double-crust pizza can be made with a carefully chosen mixture of leftovers. There must be cheese or *besciamella* to keep it moist, but you can add anchovies, cooked meat sauce, capers, olives—whatever you like, as long as their flavors suit each other.

pizza rustica

1 cake compressed fresh yeast, or
1 tablespoon active dry yeast

a pinch of sugar

1 cup warm water

2⅓ cups all-purpose flour
plus extra, for dusting

1 tablespoon olive oil, plus extra for
brushing

a pinch of salt

filling

4 oz. cubed melting cheese such as
mozzarella

3 oz. cubed salami, ham, or cooked
sausage

⅓ cup cooked chopped spinach

4 sun-dried tomatoes in oil, chopped

3–4 tablespoons tomato sauce, *Salsa
Pizzaiola* (page 139), or similar

2–3 tablespoons chopped mixed herbs

sea salt and freshly ground black pepper

a floured baking sheet

serves 2

To make the dough, put the fresh yeast and sugar in a medium bowl and beat until creamy. Whisk in the warm water and leave for 10 minutes until frothy. For other yeasts, use according to the package instructions.

Sift the flour into a large bowl and make a hollow in the center. Pour in the yeast mixture, olive oil, and a good pinch of salt. Mix with a round-bladed knife, then your hands, until the dough comes together. Transfer to a floured surface, wash and dry your hands, and knead for 10 minutes until smooth and elastic. The dough should be quite soft, but if too soft to handle, add more flour, 1 tablespoon at a time. Put the dough in a clean, oiled bowl, cover with a damp dish towel or plastic wrap, and let rise until doubled in size—about 1 hour.

To make the filling, put the mozzarella, salami, spinach, sun-dried tomatoes, tomato sauce, and mixed herbs in a bowl and season with salt and pepper.

Roll out the dough to a large circle, making sure it is well floured so it doesn't stick. Pile the filling onto one half of the dough, avoiding the edges. Flip over the other half to cover, press the edges together to seal, then twist and crimp. Slide onto a floured baking sheet and brush lightly with olive oil. Make a slash in the top or it could explode when cooking.

Bake in a preheated oven at 425°F for 25 minutes until golden and firm. Remove from the oven and set aside for about 5 minutes before serving.

Focaccia literally means "a bread that was baked on the hearth," but it is easy to bake in conventional ovens. It is found in many different forms, and can be thin and crisp, thick and soft, round or square. I make this one in a pan, but it can be shaped on a baking sheet to any shape you want. A terra cotta bakestone (*testa*) or unglazed terra cotta floor tile heated in the oven will give pizzas and *focacce* extra lift and a crisp base. Although a rustic focaccia can be made with any basic pizza dough, the secret of a truly light focaccia lies in three risings, and dimpling the dough with your fingers so it traps olive oil while it bakes. Serve with olive oil, some balsamic vinegar for dipping, and a handful of olives.

focaccia al rosmarino

5 cups Italian-style flour or all-purpose flour, plus extra for kneading

½ teaspoon fine salt

1½ cakes compressed fresh yeast (for dried yeast, follow the package instructions)

⅔ cup good olive oil

2 cups warm water

coarse sea salt

sprigs of rosemary

a water spray

2 shallow cake pans, pie or pizza plates, 10 inches diameter, lightly oiled

makes 2 thick focacce, 10 inches diameter

Sift the flour and salt into a large bowl and make a hollow in the center. Crumble in the yeast. Pour in 3 tablespoons of the olive oil, then rub in the yeast until the mixture resembles fine bread crumbs. Pour in the hot water and mix with your hands until the dough comes together.

Transfer the dough to a floured surface, wash and dry your hands, and knead for 10 minutes until smooth and elastic. The dough should be quite soft, but if too soft to handle, knead in more flour, 1 tablespoon at a time. Put the dough in a clean, oiled bowl, cover with a damp dish towel or plastic wrap, and let rise in a warm place until doubled in size, about 30 minutes–1½ hours.

Punch down the dough and cut in half. Put on a floured surface and shape each half into a round ball. Roll out into 2 circles, 10 inches diameter, and put in the pans. Cover with a damp dish towel or plastic wrap and let rise for 30 minutes.

Remove the dish towel and, using your finger tips, make dimples all over the surface of the dough. They can be quite deep. Pour over the remaining oil and sprinkle generously with salt. Cover again and let rise for 30 minutes. Spray with water, sprinkle the rosemary on top, and bake in a preheated oven at 400°F for 20–25 minutes. Transfer to a wire rack to cool. Eat the same day or freeze immediately. Serve as bread with a meal, or as a snack with oil, vinegar, and olives as suggested in the recipe introduction.

secondi piatti
e contorni

1 lb. small squid, cleaned

8 shrimp tails (optional)

2 lb. fresh mussels and clams*

3½ lb. mixed whole but cleaned fish
(see note on fish choice)

flavored broth

⅔ cup extra virgin olive oil

4 medium leeks, sliced and well washed

4 garlic cloves, finely chopped

1¼ cups dry white wine

a large pinch of saffron threads

½ lb. ripe red plum tomatoes,
coarsely chopped

2 tablespoons sun-dried tomato paste or
purée or 6 sun-dried tomatoes in oil,
drained and coarsely chopped

1 teaspoon fennel seeds

1 tablespoon dried oregano

sea salt and freshly ground black pepper

to serve

lemon wedges

handfuls of freshly chopped flat-leaf parsley

crusty bread

serves 6–8

*Scrub and debeard the mussels. Tap all
the mussels and clams against the work
surface. Discard any that don't close—they
are dead—and also any with damaged
shells. Keep in a bowl of cold water until
ready to cook.*

On Fridays and market days, fish is the best thing to buy. Cooked in a big quantity, this stew is the perfect family feast and so typical of many coastal *trattorie*. Try to include a good selection of fish—in Italy, there are boxes of fish on market stalls labeled *per zuppa*, which means small or bony fish with lots of flavor, only for soups or stews. A well-flavored base broth is essential, including saffron and fennel seeds, and the fish is then poached in this stock. The fish is served separately and the broth is ladled on top.

a big fish stew

brodetto di pesce

To make the broth, heat the olive oil in a large, deep, Dutch oven and add the leeks and garlic. Cook gently for about 5 minutes until softened. Pour in the white wine and boil rapidly until reduced by half. Add the saffron, tomatoes, tomato paste, fennel seeds, and oregano. Pour in 2¾ cups water and bring to a boil. Turn down the heat, cover and simmer for 20 minutes until the tomatoes and oil separate.

Start cooking the fish. Add the squid to the pan and poach for 3–4 minutes. Remove with a slotted spoon, put on a plate, cover, and keep them warm. Add the shrimp, if using, and simmer just until opaque. Remove with a slotted spoon and keep warm with the squid. Add the mussels and clams to the broth, cover, and boil for a few minutes until they open. Remove with a slotted spoon and keep them warm. Discard any that haven't opened.

Poach all the remaining fish until just cooked, remove from the broth, arrange on a serving dish, and set the mussels, squid and shrimp on top. Taste the broth, which will have all the flavors of the cooked fish in it, and add salt and pepper if necessary. Moisten the fish with some broth and serve the rest separately with the lemon wedges, parsley, and lots of crusty bread.

Fish choice Choose at least 4 varieties—the greater the variety, the more intense the flavor. Do not choose oily fish like salmon or bluefish. Choose from: cod, grouper, halibut, monkfish, sea bass, shark, swordfish, tilefish, whiting, clams, mussels, lobster, shrimp, or squid.

Sea bass has a wonderful, clean, fresh taste and baking in parchment is the best way to cook whole fish (with the possible exception of grilling over embers). The parchment lets the fish steam in its own juices, absorbing the aroma of the fresh herbs and lemon. This cooking time should be perfect—the fish is better slightly underdone at the bone than overdone. The packages should be opened at the table to appreciate the full aroma.

sea bass baked in parchment

branzino al cartoccio

2 sea bass, about 12 oz. each, cleaned and scaled

about 1 tablespoon olive oil

4 fresh bay leaves

2 sprigs of thyme

6 thin slices of lemon

about 2 tablespoons dry white wine or freshly squeezed lemon juice

sea salt and freshly ground black pepper

baking parchment

a baking tray

serves 2

Cut 2 large rectangles of parchment paper big enough to wrap each fish generously. Brush the rectangles with a little oil.

Season the cavities of the fish with salt and pepper. Put 2 bay leaves in each one and tuck in the thyme and lemon slices.

Put one fish on one half of the paper, sprinkle with white wine or lemon juice, fold over the other half loosely, and twist or fold the edges tightly together to seal. Repeat with the other fish, then put both packages on the baking tray.

Bake in a preheated oven at 375°F for 20 minutes. Serve immediately, opening the packages at the table.

The smell of silvery blue sardines on a grill is unmistakable—it is one of the most appetizing scents in outdoor cooking. Sardines grill very well because they are an oily fish and are self-basting. Great shoals of them are to be found in Mediterranean waters in May and June, which is the best time to eat them. They are eaten grilled or fried, boned or stuffed, always *con gusto!*

grilled sardines
with salmoriglio sauce

sarde alla griglia con salmoriglio

12 fresh fat sardines

olive oil

lemon wedges, to serve

salmoriglio sauce

2 tablespoons red wine vinegar

1–2 teaspoons sugar

finely grated zest and freshly squeezed juice of ½ unwaxed lemon

¼ cup good olive oil

1 garlic clove, finely chopped

1 tablespoon crumbled dried oregano

1 tablespoon salted capers, rinsed and chopped

a grill rack

serves 4

To make the salmoriglio, put the vinegar and sugar in a bowl and stir to dissolve. Add the lemon zest and juice. Whisk in the olive oil, then add the garlic, oregano, and capers. Set aside to infuse.

Using the back of a knife, scale the sardines, starting from the tail and working towards the head. Slit open the belly and remove the insides, then rinse the fish and pat dry. Clip off any fins you don't want to see. Paint the fish with olive oil and arrange on a grill rack (there are racks especially made in a wheel shape for sardines).

Cook under a hot broiler or over glowing hot coals for about 3 minutes per side until sizzling hot and charring. Serve with the *salmoriglio* spooned over the top, with lots of lemon wedges alongside.

This dish originated in Venice during the Renaissance and has been cooked and served on gondolas on the eve of the Feast of the Redeemer in July ever since. As well as adding flavor to the delicate fish, the marinade slightly preserves it too. I have eaten this simple dish beside the Venetian lagoon with a big basket of bread and crisp, throat-tingling white wine, watching the mirage of the water meeting the sky. This dish can also be made with sardines, but sole is popular in Venice.

fillets of sole
in sweet and sour onion marinade

sogliole in saor

8 sole fillets, skinned

all-purpose flour, for dusting

½ cup olive oil

sea salt and freshly ground black pepper

saor marinade

¼ cup olive oil

2 mild onions, finely sliced

3 bay leaves or a sprig

¼ cup white wine vinegar

serves 4

To make the marinade, heat the olive oil in a skillet over medium heat. Add the onions and bay leaves. Cook, stirring, for 15–20 minutes. The onions should be softened and translucent and not browned at all. Add the vinegar and boil rapidly for a few minutes until amalgamated with the onion juices. Remove from the heat, pour into a bowl, and set aside.

Season the sole fillets with salt, and dip them in flour to coat both sides, shaking to remove the excess. Heat the olive oil in a skillet and cook the sole fillets for about 1 minute on each side. Remove and drain on paper towels.

Spoon half of the cooked and cooled marinade into a shallow dish, season with pepper, and arrange the sole fillets on top. Pour in the remaining marinade, cover with plastic wrap, and let marinate for several hours or overnight in the refrigerator. Serve at room temperature with a salad.

Tuna is a very rich meat and is always cut thinly in Italy—never as the thick seared steaks we are used to. Marinating the slices in mustard and grappa gives them a piquant crust—so good with the sweet bell peppers. Overcooking tuna can make it very dry, so watch it like a hawk.

grilled tuna steaks
with peperonata

tonno alla griglia con peperonata

4 tuna loin steaks cut ½ inch thick

olive oil, for cooking

marinade

4 garlic cloves

3 tablespoons Dijon mustard

2 tablespoons grappa or brandy

sea salt and freshly ground black pepper

peperonata

⅓ cup olive oil

2 lb. fresh ripe tomatoes, peeled, halved, seeded, and chopped, or 28 oz. canned chopped tomatoes

½ teaspoon hot red pepper flakes

2 medium onions, finely sliced

3 garlic cloves, chopped

3 large red bell peppers, halved, seeded, and cut into thin strips

sea salt and freshly ground black pepper

serves 4

To make the marinade, crush the garlic, put in a bowl, and beat in the mustard and grappa. Season with salt and pepper and use to spread over the cut sides of the tuna. Arrange in a non-metal dish, cover, and let marinate in a cool place for about 1 hour.

To make the peperonata, heat 3 tablespoons of the oil in a saucepan, then add the tomatoes and pepper flakes. Cook over medium heat for 10 minutes, or until the tomatoes disintegrate.

Heat the remaining oil in a skillet, add the onions, garlic, and peppers and sauté for about 10 minutes until softening. Add the pepper mixture to the tomatoes and simmer, covered, for 45 minutes until very soft. Taste and season with salt and pepper.

Preheat the grill or broiler. Sprinkle the steaks with olive oil and arrange on a rack over a foil-lined broiler pan. Broil for about 2 minutes on each side until crusty on the outside and still pink in the middle. Alternatively, grill over hot embers for slightly less time. Serve with the peperonata, which can be served hot or cold.

Chicken and small game birds are very popular cooked this way. They are "spatchcocked"—that is split open and flattened, so they cook evenly. Many *trattorie* cook *alla brace*—over hot coals in the hearth. To make the charcoal, a wood fire is lit, and when the wood has turned to glowing red ashes, they are spread out in an even layer and left until white on top. A low iron grill on legs is placed over the coals and the spatchcocked birds cooked on top. The smell is wonderful as they sizzle over the coals. Why *alla diavola*? The cooked spatchcocked bird is said to look like the shape of the devil's face (the legs being the horns), the charring is the color of the devil, and the chile makes it hotter than hell! The best way to eat these is with your fingers.

devilled grilled chicken

pollo alla diavola

1 medium chicken, about 1.5 kg

200 ml olive oil

freshly squeezed juice of 1 lemon

2 garlic cloves, crushed

1 teaspoon hot red pepper flakes

sea salt and freshly ground black pepper

lemon wedges, to serve

a metal mesh grill basket

serves 4

Turn the chicken breast side down. You will see the backbone underneath the skin. Take a pair of kitchen shears and cut along one side of the backbone. Cut along the other side and you will have removed the backbone completely. Turn the bird over breast side up and open out. Press down hard on the breastbone until you hear a crack and the bird flattens out.

Put the olive oil in a bowl, add the lemon juice, garlic, pepper flakes, a good pinch of salt, and lots of pepper. Mix well. Pour the mixture into a shallow dish, add the chicken, and turn in the marinade to coat. Cover and let marinate in the refrigerator for at least 1 hour, or overnight.

Remove the chicken from the marinade and set it flat on one side of a mesh grill basket. Clamp the basket shut. Grill or broil bone side first for 20 minutes. Turn it over, lower the heat, and cook for 20–30 minutes until cooked through and blackened but not burnt. Baste with the marinade from time to time. Serve hot with lemon wedges.

This is one of the most famous dishes to come out of Piedmont, and still a favorite. It is delightful made with turkey instead of veal if you prefer. Turkey is popular in Italy, and if cooked and cooled in the poaching liquid, it will remain nice and moist. This is a very soothing dish.

vitello tonnato

2 lb. tenderloin of veal or turkey breast

2¾ cups dry white wine

1 celery stalk, chopped

1 carrot, chopped

1 small onion, chopped

1 bay leaf

3 cloves

tuna mayonnaise

8 oz. canned tuna in oil, drained

6 anchovies in oil, rinsed

1 tablespoon capers, rinsed, plus extra to serve

2 hard-cooked egg yolks

1¼ cups olive oil

freshly squeezed juice of 1 lemon

2 teaspoons white wine vinegar

sea salt and freshly ground black pepper

to serve

thin lemon slices

a few parsley sprigs

kitchen twine

serves 6–8

Two days before serving, put the veal or turkey in a bowl with the wine, celery, carrot, onion, bay leaf, and cloves, mix well, and let marinate in the refrigerator for 24 hours.

Remove the meat from the marinade and tie up neatly with fine twine. If using turkey, remove the skin. Put in a saucepan just large enough to hold it. Pour in the marinade, then top up with water until the meat is just covered. Cover with a lid, bring to a boil, then reduce the heat, and simmer very slowly for about 1¼ hours or until cooked through. When cooked, remove from the heat and let cool in the liquid.

When cold, remove the meat from the liquid, wrap and chill the meat, and strain the liquid. Chill the liquid for a couple of hours to set any grease. Lift off and discard any grease and set the liquid aside.

To make the mayonnaise, put the tuna, anchovies, capers, and hard-cooked egg yolks in a blender or food processor and blend until smooth. With the machine running, pour in the olive oil in a thin stream until it has all been absorbed and the mixture thick and homogenized. Scrape out into a bowl and season to taste with the lemon juice and vinegar.

Using the poaching liquid, carefully dilute the sauce until it is the right flowing consistency. Taste and adjust the seasoning with salt and pepper. Slice the veal or turkey thinly. Spread a few tablespoons of the sauce on a large, flat serving dish. Add a layer of veal, coat with the sauce, and continue until all is used up, ending with sauce. Sprinkle some extra capers on top, add the slices of lemon and a few parsley sprigs and serve immediately.

A magnificent way to cook lamb long and slowly, especially if it is not as young as it might be. Liver is often served with onions cooked to melting sweetness, and this is a similar technique. The black olives enrich the dish and give it a smoky taste. The chops can be finished off in a medium hot oven instead of cooking on top. They are very good reheated.

braised lamb chops
with onions, herbs, and olives

costolette di agnello con cipolle e olive

8–12 lamb chops, depending on size

½ cup olive oil

2 lb. onions, finely sliced

2 tablespoons chopped fresh oregano and rosemary, mixed

4 anchovies in oil, drained, rinsed and chopped

15 black olives, pitted

sea salt and freshly ground black pepper

rosemary sprigs, to serve

serves 4

Season the meat on both sides with salt and pepper.

Heat half the oil in a large sauté pan until very hot, then add the chops and quickly brown on both sides. Remove to a plate and let cool.

Heat the remaining oil in the same pan and add the onions. Cook gently for 15 minutes, stirring occasionally, until the onions begin to soften–do not let them brown. Stir in the herbs, anchovies, olives, salt, and pepper.

Arrange the chops on top of the bed of onions and cover with a lid. Cook over very low heat for 20 minutes, watching that the onions don't catch and burn. Serve topped with rosemary sprigs.

Italians love meat cooked very rare: you will often see a slip of a girl tucking into a steak that would comfortably feed two—and she will eat it all. The steaks are produced from the huge, handsome, white Chianina cattle, native to Tuscany. A great place to taste real Tuscan beef simply cooked over wood embers is at Ristorante dei Laghi, near Civitella, which is a carnivore's paradise—family run, warm and welcoming, and full of hunters' stuffed trophies.

beefsteak with arugula

tagliata con la rucola

4 T-bone steaks, about 8 oz. each

2 tablespoons olive oil

8 oz. arugula

sea salt and freshly ground black pepper

chopped fresh parsley, serve

serves 4

Brush the steaks with olive oil and season very well with salt and pepper. Heat a stove-top grill pan or light an outdoor grill. When the pan is smoking hot, add the steaks and cook for 2 minutes on each side to seal, then lower the heat and continue to cook for about 4 minutes per side for medium-rare steaks, less for rare.

Transfer the steaks to a cutting board, cut the meat from the bone, and slice it thickly. Put a pile of arugula on 4 warm plates and arrange the sliced meat on top. Pour any juices from the steaks onto the meat and serve immediately, topped with chopped parsley.

A simple way to give ordinary chicken or rabbit all the taste of the wild hills. The secret is in the reduction of the wine and the long, slow cooking. Farmed rabbits are huge in Italy and come with everything attached, which really adds to the sauce. Expect this dish to have a rich sauce of tomato, herbs, and perhaps mushrooms— all available to the hunter on his expedition into the wild. The sauce is very dark and rich, so serve with plain fare such as polenta or just a salad afterwards.

hunter's-style rabbit stew

coniglio alla cacciatora

1 medium chicken, about 3 lb.,
or 1 large rabbit (liver kept),
cut into 8 pieces

4 large garlic cloves, finely chopped

1 tablespoon finely chopped rosemary

1 teaspoon salt

1 teaspoon cracked black pepper

1 oz. dried porcini mushrooms

1 bottle dry red wine (750 ml)

2 sprigs of rosemary

3 tablespoons olive oil

2 tablespoons balsamic vinegar

2 tablespoons sun-dried tomato paste
or tomato purée

14 oz. canned chopped tomatoes

chicken stock or water (see method)

sea salt and freshly ground black pepper

polenta, to serve (page 51)

serves 4

Wash and dry the chicken or rabbit pieces. Put the garlic, rosemary, salt, and pepper in a bowl, mix well, then rub it into the flesh, especially the cut sides. Cover and let marinate for 2 hours in a cool place or longer in the refrigerator.

Soak the porcini mushrooms in warm water for at least 20 minutes. Meanwhile pour the wine into a non-reactive pan, add the rosemary sprigs, and boil hard until reduced by half. Strain and cool.

Heat the oil in a large skillet and sauté the chicken or rabbit, until well browned all over. Remove to a casserole. If using rabbit, add the liver to the pan, sauté until golden, then add to the casserole.

Deglaze the pan with the balsamic vinegar, then add the cooled wine, scraping up the sediment. Whisk in the tomato paste, tomatoes, and add the mushrooms and their soaking water. Season with salt and pepper, bring to a boil, and pour over the chicken or rabbit. Add a little water or stock so the liquid just covers the meat. Bring to a boil, then cover and simmer very gently for 45 minutes–1 hour.

Lift the chicken or rabbit to a warm serving dish. Mash the liver, if using, into the sauce and reduce, if necessary, by boiling fast to a syrupy consistency. Pour the sauce over the meat and serve with polenta.

Meatballs in tomato sauce are so much part of Italian food culture that they have to be in this book. These are bursting with flavor from fennel seeds and garlic. When cooked, it is common practice to serve the sauce with pasta as an appetizer, followed by the meatballs and maybe a vegetable. If you make the *polpette* very small, you can serve them in sauce with spaghetti. The meat can also be cooked as a *polpettone*—rolled into one large piece, and simmered for a couple of hours. In this case, the sauce is certainly used to dress pasta first and the meat is sliced and served as a separate course. This recipe can also be used minus the fennel and chile to make fresh Italian sausage meat if you find Italian sausages difficult to buy.

pork and fennel meatballs
in tomato sauce

polpette al finocchio in ragù

1 lb. shoulder or leg of pork

8 oz. piece of unsmoked ham

8 oz. boneless pork chops, with fat

2 garlic cloves, crushed

2 tablespoon fennel seeds

a large pinch of hot red pepper flakes

2 teaspoons sea salt

1 tablespoon sugar

2 tablespoons coarsely crushed black pepper

olive oil (see method)

⅔ cup dry white wine

14 oz. canned chopped tomatoes

½ cup tomato passata (strained crushed tomatoes)

sea salt and freshly ground black pepper

serves 6

Trim the shoulder of pork, ham and pork chops of any skin or connective tissue. Cut the meat into large chunks, pass them through the coarse blade of an electric grinder or chop very finely with a large sharp knife or cleaver (do not use a food processor).

Put the meat in a large bowl, add the garlic, fennel seeds, pepper flakes, salt, sugar, and pepper. Mix with clean hands or a large wooden spoon. At this stage, the sausage meat is ready to use, but you can cover the bowl and let it mature in the refrigerator overnight.

With dampened hands, shape into meatballs about the size of a walnut. To cook, heat 2 tablespoons of the oil in a skillet and quickly brown the meatballs all over, in batches if necessary. Remove to a plate with a slotted spoon and add the wine. Deglaze the pan and let the wine bubble until there is only 1 tablespoon left. Add the canned tomatoes and passata, salt, and pepper. Bring back to a boil, then return the meatballs to the sauce. Partially cover with a lid and simmer for 30–40 minutes, topping up with water if the sauce is becoming too dry. Serve as it is or dress some pasta with the sauce as an appetizer and eat the meatballs as a course on their own (see recipe introduction above).

The Tuscans have a reputation for being great game hunters. In the past, when they used to cook little gamebirds, or *uccelletti*, they would generally season them with sage. Although this dish contains no *uccelletti*, it is cooked in the same way—the sausages take the place of the birds. This is the most famous of the hundreds of ways to cook beans and is equally delicious served with roast pork—or even a homemade hamburger.

grilled sausages
with tomato and sage bean stew

salsicce con fagioli all'uccelletto

1 lb. dried cannellini or haricot beans or other white beans, or, if lucky, 2 lb. fresh cannellini or borlotti beans

a pinch of baking soda

8 fat fresh Italian-style sausages

⅓ cup olive oil

3 garlic cloves, crushed

about 10 fresh sage leaves

12 oz. fresh ripe tomatoes, peeled, seeded, and puréed, or 1¼ cups tomato passata (strained, crushed tomatoes)

sea salt and freshly ground black pepper

serves 4

If using dried beans, cover with plenty of cold water and soak overnight. The next day, drain and rinse them, then cook in plenty of boiling water without any salt, but with a pinch of baking soda (to keep the skins soft) for about 1–1½ hours, or until tender. Drain. If using fresh beans, shell and boil them in slightly salted water until ready, 25–30 minutes, then drain.

Brush the sausages with oil and grill or broil for 15 minutes until tender and crisp on the outside.

Meanwhile, heat the oil in a saucepan and add the garlic, sage, and black pepper. Fry until the garlic is golden and the sage beginning to become transparent and crisp. Remove and reserve a few crisp leaves for serving.

Add the puréed tomatoes, heat to simmering, then add the cooked beans. Cook for 10 minutes, then taste and adjust the seasoning with salt and pepper. Serve the sausages with the beans.

If you ask for a mixed salad in Italy, this is what you will get. Don't be surprised if the tomatoes are not red ripe, but hard and green—this is how they are eaten in salads. If you think about it, this dish is to cleanse the palate after a meat or fish course, and that is just what it does. Leaving the skins on potatoes and tomatoes is generally not done, but you can do it at home. Salads do not come dressed—bottles of oil and vinegar are given to you so that you may dress your own. The vinegar is often red wine vinegar; balsamic vinegar is not likely to appear in a trattoria.

italian mixed salad

insalata mista

12 oz. salad potatoes, peeled

6 oz. fine green beans, trimmed

extra virgin olive oil

¼ cup black or green olives, pitted

1 small crisp lettuce

2 large ripe tomatoes, quartered (or unripe to be authentic)

3 tablespoons chopped fresh parsley

sea salt and freshly ground black pepper

to serve

a small bottle of good olive oil

a small bottle of red wine vinegar

serves 4

Boil the potatoes in salted water for about 15 minutes or until tender, adding the beans 4 minutes before the potatoes are ready. Drain and cover with cold water to stop the cooking.

When cold, drain well. Remove the beans to a bowl, slice the potatoes thickly, and add to the beans, moistening with a little olive oil. Add the olives and toss well.

Wash the lettuce and tear into bite-size pieces. Add the lettuce and tomatoes to the potatoes and beans and toss lightly. Transfer to a serving bowl and sprinkle with parsley, salt, and pepper. Serve the olive oil and vinegar separately and dress the salad at the table.

In Sicily, the land of orange and lemon groves, this salad is often served after grilled fish—especially in the region around Palermo. It is another example of their passion for sweet and savory combinations and is very refreshing.

orange, frisée, and black olive salad

insalata di arance, indivia e olive nere

2 oranges

1 red onion

4 oz. frisée or escarole

dressing

finely grated zest and juice of
1 unwaxed orange

⅓ cup extra virgin olive oil

2 tablespoons finely sliced fresh basil

2 tablespoons finely chopped, pitted,
Greek-style, oven-dried black olives

2 sun-dried tomatoes in oil, finely chopped

sea salt and freshly ground black pepper

serves 4

To make the dressing, put the orange zest and juice, olive oil, basil, olives, and sun-dried tomatoes in a large bowl. Mix well, season with salt and pepper, and set aside to develop the flavors.

Peel the oranges with a sharp knife, removing all the skin and white pith. Cut out the segments. Set aside in a bowl. Finely slice the onion, using a very sharp, thin-bladed knife or a Japanese mandolin. Immediately toss the onion and oranges in the dressing to prevent discoloration. Let marinate in a cool place for 15 minutes.

Put the frisée on a plate and pile the dressed orange and onion mixture in the center, spooning over any remaining dressing. Serve immediately.

The fennel absorbs all the flavors of the olive oil, lemon juice, and chile and the anchovy adds a salty touch. Braising the fennel slowly makes it meltingly soft and tender with a hint of aniseed. This is delicious with pork dishes and more robust fish like swordfish. Again, this is another of those dishes you can make in advance and it only improves with keeping.

stewed fennel
with olive oil, lemon, and chile

finocchi alla diavola

4 medium heads of fennel

1 cup extra virgin olive oil

finely grated zest and juice of 1 large unwaxed lemon

1 anchovy in oil or salt, rinsed and finely chopped

½ teaspoon hot red pepper flakes

a little white wine vinegar (optional)

sea salt and freshly ground black pepper

serves 4–6

Trim the stalks and fronds from the fennel. Discard the stalks, but keep the green fronds. Halve the fennel bulbs. Cut out the hard core, then cut each half into 2 wedges. Arrange in a flameproof baking dish.

Put the olive oil, lemon zest and juice, anchovy, pepper flakes, vinegar, if using, salt, and pepper in a bowl and whisk well. Pour over the fennel. Bring the dish to a boil on top of the stove. Cover with foil and bake in a preheated oven at 325°F for 1 hour or until very soft and tender.

Remove from the oven and remove the foil. Taste the liquid and add a dash of vinegar to sharpen it if necessary. Serve warm or cold, sprinkled with the reserved fennel fronds.

This is better the next day after the flavors have matured.

Plum tomatoes are perfect for roasting as they have a low moisture content, have less tendency to burst, and remain quite meaty. This recipe, along with plain boiled green beans tossed in olive oil, is one of the most popular side dishes in Italian trattorias. I have buried whole garlic cloves in the center, which perfume the entire tomato and softens to a silky texture.

roasted tomatoes
with a secret

pomodori al forno

6 large ripe plum or round tomatoes, with their stalks on if possible

6 small garlic cloves, peeled

extra virgin olive oil

sea salt and freshly ground black pepper

a baking dish

serves 6

Cut a thin sliver off the base of each tomato so it will stand upright. Cut off the tops and push a garlic clove deep inside each tomato. Season with salt and pepper and replace the tops.

Lightly oil a baking dish and add the tomatoes upright and close together. Sprinkle with olive oil and season again with salt and pepper. Bake in a preheated oven at 325°F for about 2 hours, checking every now and then. They should be slightly shriveled, and a brilliant red color. Take them out and insert a sharp knife in the middle to see if the garlic clove is soft—it must be very soft. Replace the tops and serve hot or cold.

My friend Louise, who lives in Italy, goes completely crazy for this dish. She always persuades me to put it on the menu for my guests on our cooking course in Tuscany, but it's really for her. It is very rich and deserves to be eaten on its own. It is said to originate in Campania and is often confused with *melanzane alla Parmigiana* which is another dish altogether. Sometimes it is layered with hard-cooked eggs, but I like it better without. This is easily prepared in advance and refrigerated to put in the oven at a moment's notice. It is very well behaved, making it a popular dish with the trattoria proprietor.

baked eggplant, tomato, mozzarella, and parmesan

parmigiana di melanzane

4 medium eggplant

2 tablespoons olive oil, plus extra for the eggplant

1 small onion, finely chopped

28 oz. canned chopped tomatoes, drained

2 tablespoons chopped fresh basil

½–¾ cup freshly grated Parmesan cheese

8 oz. fresh mozzarella cheese, thinly sliced

sea salt and freshly ground black pepper

a shallow oven dish, 10 inches diameter, lightly oiled

serves 4

Cut the eggplant lengthwise into strips ½ inch wide. Soak them for 30 minutes in a bowl of salted water.

Heat the oil in a skillet, add the onion, and cook for 5 minutes until softening, then add the tomatoes and basil and simmer gently for 30 minutes. Season with salt and pepper.

Drain the eggplant, then rinse and pat dry. Sauté them or brush with olive oil and roast in a preheated oven at 350°F for about 20 minutes until deep golden brown. Set aside.

Arrange the eggplant in a single layer in the oven dish, then add a layer of grated Parmesan, followed by a layer of sliced mozzarella and a layer of the tomato sauce. Continue layering in this order until all the ingredients have been used, ending with a sauce layer (this will keep the dish moist—if you want a crisp top, end with eggplant and Parmesan).

Bake in the oven at 350°F for 30–35 minutes until browned and bubbling. Remove and set aside for 10 minutes to settle before serving. Serve warm or at room temperature.

You will often see this dish on Italian menus, and it usually means that the mushrooms are sliced and sautéed, then finished off with the reduction of wine and olive oil. This is good if the mushrooms are small, but when it is mushroom season and you have the opportunity of cooking larger mushrooms, this is the way to do it. I have seen them being grilled over a bed of charcoal and the smell was fantastic.

broiled and sautéed mushrooms

funghi trifolati

4 large portobello or 4 large fresh porcini mushrooms

olive oil (see method)

1 cup white wine

2 garlic cloves, chopped

freshly squeezed juice of 1 lemon

3 tablespoons chopped fresh parsley

sea salt and freshly ground black pepper

serves 4

Pull the stalks off the mushrooms, then arrange the caps open side up on an oiled broiler pan. Chop the stalks finely and set aside. Brush the mushrooms with olive oil, season with salt and pepper, and cook under a preheated broiler for 5 minutes.

Meanwhile, put 3 tablespoons olive oil in a skillet with the white wine, garlic, lemon juice, parsley, and the reserved chopped stalks. Bring to a boil, then boil hard to reduce by half. Season well with salt and pepper and remove from the heat. Transfer the mushrooms to warm serving plates, then pour the sauce over the top. Serve immediately.

dolci e
digestivi

The secret of a great panna cotta is in the wobble. I have eaten many indifferent versions—some of them made from package mixes. This one is really good. *Panna cotta* means "cooked or scalded cream" and is said to have originated in Piedmont or Lombardy, where the cream and milk are very rich.

panna cotta
with candied orange zest

2 cups heavy cream

1¼ cups whole milk

1 vanilla bean, split

¼ cup sugar

3 teaspoons powdered gelatin*

candied orange zest

2 unwaxed oranges

¼ cup sugar

6 molds, about ½ cup each

serves 6

*Panna cotta must be wobbly. However, if you are nervous about inverting them, use 4 teaspoons gelatin. They will melt if the dipping water is too hot.

To make the panna cotta, put the cream and milk, split vanilla bean, and sugar in a saucepan and bring to a boil. Crumble or sprinkle the gelatin into the cream and stir until dissolved. Cool, then chill in the refrigerator until it JUST begins to thicken. At this stage, stir the cream briskly to distribute the vanilla seeds, then remove the vanilla bean. (Rinse and dry and keep in the sugar jar.) Pour into 6 individual molds, set on a tray, and refrigerate for at least 5 hours or until set.

Remove the zest from the oranges with a sharp potato peeler (removing any bitter white pith with a knife afterwards). Cut the zest into long, fine shreds. Bring a small saucepan of water to a boil and blanch the shreds for 1 minute. Drain, then refresh in cold water.

Put the sugar and ½ cup water in a small saucepan and stir until dissolved. Add the orange shreds and bring to a rolling boil. Boil for 2–3 minutes, then strain the shreds through a sieve and transfer to a plate to cool. Before they cool too much, separate them a little so they don't stick together.

To serve, press the top of the panna cotta and gently pull away from the edge of the mold (this breaks the airlock). Carefully invert onto a small cold plate. (Give the mold a good shake and the panna cotta should drop out.) If it still won't turn out, dip very briefly into warm water, then invert onto the plate again and lift off. Top with the orange shreds and a spoonful of syrup.

At last, an ice cream that actually tastes like a real Italian gelato. There is no cream and no eggs, so no custard making. It is silky smooth and heavenly, served in a glass *coppa* with delicious warmed Amarena cherries. Amarena cherries are sold in pretty white and blue glass jars—a great souvenir of a holiday—but are less expensive bought in cans from an Italian gourmet store.

vanilla gelato
with hot cherry sauce

gelato alla vaniglia con amarene

1 vanilla bean

5 cups whole milk

2 tablespoons non-fat dry milk

¼ cup cornstarch or wheat starch

1⅓ cups sugar

1 teaspoon pure vanilla extract

13 oz. canned Italian Amarena cherries in syrup

2 tablespoons maraschino or kirsch

an ice cream maker

serves 6

Split the vanilla bean in two and put in a saucepan with 4 cups of the milk. Whisk in the dry milk. Bring to boiling point, turn off the heat, and leave to infuse for 20 minutes.

Remove the vanilla bean and scrape out the seeds into the milk. Whisk the seeds through the milk. Wash and dry the bean and store in the sugar jar.

Dissolve the cornstarch in the remaining milk, then pour into the hot milk and add the sugar. Set over the heat again and bring to a boil, stirring constantly until thickened. Cover the surface with plastic wrap and let cool to room temperature. Stir in the vanilla extract. Chill, then churn in an ice cream maker.

Alternatively, pour into a shallow freezer tray and freeze until is frozen around the edges. Mash well with a fork. When it is half-frozen again, blend in a food processor until creamy, then cover and freeze until firm. Let soften in the refrigerator for 20 minutes before serving.

When ready to serve, put the cherries, their syrup, and the liqueur in a saucepan and heat gently. Serve the ice cream in large scoops with the sauce trickled over it.

It's worth making a journey to Italy just to taste lemons that have been properly ripened in the sun. Walk through a lemon grove when the glossy green trees are in blossom and the scent is intoxicating. The beautiful leaves can be used like bay leaves or the more exotic Thai lime leaves to impart a lemony flavor to sweet and savory dishes alike. I mix the orange with the lemon juice, because it softens the acidity of some un-sunkissed lemons.

sorbetto al limone

1½ cups sugar

finely grated zest and juice of 6 unwaxed lemons, plus 6 medium, even-size lemons

finely grated zest and juice of 1 unwaxed orange

an ice cream maker

serves 6: makes about 1 quart

Put the sugar and 2¾ cups water in a saucepan with the lemon and orange zest. Bring slowly to a boil and boil rapidly for 3–4 minutes. Remove from the heat, and let cool. Meanwhile, strain the fruit juices into a bowl. When the syrup is cold, strain into the bowl of juice. Chill. When cold, churn in an ice cream maker.

Meanwhile, cut the tops off the remaining 6 lemons and shave a little off each base so that it will stand up. Scoop out the insides (squeeze and keep the juice for another time. Put in the freezer. When the sorbet is frozen, fill the lemon shells and set the tops back on. Replace in the freezer until needed. Soften in the refrigerator for 10–15 minutes before serving.

Tasting this on a stifling hot, thundery night in Venice, I thought I had died and gone to heaven. The trattoria was full and it was somebody's birthday—frosty glasses of this alcoholic sherbet were brought to the happy table at the end of the meal. I had to have one too, and was very glad. Not only did it hit the spot, but I felt quite shivery as the frozen liquid slid down my throat. This makes a perfect end to a meal or, if you like, a refreshing break during a multicourse dinner.

scroppino

6 scoops of lemon sorbet, preferably homemade (page 117)

¼ cup frozen vodka

1 cup chilled good prosecco (Venetian sparkling wine) or other dry sparkling wine

4 glasses, preferably Champagne flutes or saucers

serves 4

Put the 4 glasses in the freezer well beforehand.

For the best results, you should use a blender and make sure all the ingredients and the bowl and pitcher are very cold, as well as the glasses.

Put the lemon sorbet, vodka, and prosecco in a blender and blend to a sludgy, frothy consistency. Scoop into the glasses and serve with spoons.

There is nothing quite as sensual as warm zabaglione served straight from the pan. Many like to beat it in a copper bowl so that it cooks quickly. The secret is not to let the mixture get too hot, but still hot enough to cook and thicken the egg yolks. The proportions are easy to remember: one egg yolk to one tablespoon sugar to one tablespoon Marsala, serves one person. It must be made at the last moment, but it doesn't take long and is well worth the effort.

zabaglione

2 large egg yolks

2 tablespoons sweet Marsala wine

2 tablespoons sugar

savoiardi or ladyfingers, for dipping

serves 2

Put the egg yolks, Marsala, and sugar in a medium heatproof bowl (preferably copper or stainless steel) and beat with a hand-held electric mixer or a whisk until well blended.

Set the bowl over a saucepan of gently simmering water—the bottom should at no time be in contact with the water. Do not let the water boil. Whisk the mixture until it is glossy, pale, light, and fluffy and holds a trail when dropped from the whisk. This should take about 5 minutes. Serve immediately in warmed cocktail glasses with ladyfingers for dipping.

Variation To make chilled zabaglione for two, when cooked, remove the bowl from the heat and whisk until completely cold. In a separate bowl, whisk ⅔ cup heavy cream until floppy, then fold into the cold zabaglione. Spoon into glasses and chill for 2–3 hours.

A refreshing change from the classic French *tarte au citron*. The almonds give the tart more body and add another flavor dimension. Traditionally, this is made with freshly ground almonds, because they have a fine, creamy texture and a better flavor than the ready-ground kind, which are difficult to find in Italy. If you'd like to try this method, grind the same weight of whole blanched almonds with half the sugar to prevent them becoming oily. Beat the eggs with the remaining sugar then stir in the ground sugar and almonds.

lemon and almond tart

torta di limone e mandorle

pasta frolla (shortcrust pastry)

2 sticks butter

2 cups all-purpose flour

½ cup sugar

2 egg yolks

lemon and almond filling

4 extra-large eggs, lightly beaten

⅔ cup sugar

finely grated zest and freshly squeezed juice of 3 unwaxed lemons

1 stick unsalted butter, melted

¾ cup flaked almonds, ground to a powder in a blender

whipped cream, to serve

a fluted tart pan, 9 inches diameter

foil and baking beans

a baking sheet

serves 8

To make the *pasta frolla*, work the butter into the flour and sugar until it looks like grated Parmesan cheese.

Put the 2 egg yolks in a small bowl, add 1 tablespoon water, and beat lightly. Add to the flour mixture and knead lightly until smooth. Knead into a ball, flatten, then wrap in plastic wrap and let it rest for 30 minutes.

Roll out the dough on a floured surface and use to line the tart pan. Prick the base all over with a fork, then chill or freeze for 15 minutes to set the dough. Line with foil, flicking the edges inwards towards the center so that it doesn't catch on the dough. Fill with baking beans, set on the baking sheet and bake blind in the center of a preheated oven at 375°F for 10–12 minutes.

Remove the foil and beans and return the pie crust to the oven for a further 5–7 minutes to dry out completely.

To make the filling, put the eggs, sugar, lemon zest, and juice in a bowl and whisk until light and fluffy. Stir in the melted butter and almonds. Mix well and pour into the prepared pie crust. Bake for 25–30 minutes, until the crust and the top of the tart is golden brown. Cool, then chill before serving with whipped cream.

You'll find simple tarts made with seasonal fruit all over Italy. Unless the trattoria has a talented baker behind the scenes, tarts will be bought in from a local *pasticceria*. The ricotta makes a lovely light cheesecake with a slightly grainy texture. Be sure to try this only with fresh figs—dried are not the same. If figs aren't in season, all sorts of other fruits can be used to top the tart.

caramelized fig tart

crostata di fichi

6 tablespoons butter, softened

6 tablespoons sugar

3 egg yolks

½ teaspoon pure vanilla extract

1 cup plus 2 tablespoons all-purpose flour, plus extra for dusting

1 teaspoon salt

1 egg yolk, beaten, for brushing

fig filling

8 oz. fresh ricotta cheese (1 cup)

1 stick plus 1 tablespoon butter, softened

⅔ cup sugar or vanilla sugar

2 eggs

8–10 ripe black figs (depending on size), cut in halves or quarters

raspberry jelly

wax paper

a false-bottom tart pan, 8 inches diameter

foil and baking beans

a baking sheet

serves 6

To make the dough, put the butter, sugar, the 3 egg yolks, and vanilla in a food processor and blend until smooth.

Sift the flour and salt onto a sheet of wax paper. Shoot the flour into the food processor and blend until just mixed.

Transfer to a floured work surface and knead gently until smooth. Form into a ball, flatten and wrap in plastic wrap. Chill for at least 30 minutes.

To make the filling, put the cheese, butter, and sugar in a bowl and beat until smooth. Put the 2 eggs in another bowl, beat well, then gradually beat them into the cheese mixture. Set aside.

Roll out the dough thinly and use to line the tart pan. Prick the base all over with a fork, then chill oir freeze for 15 miutes to set the dough. Line with foil and baking beans, set on a baking sheet, and bake blind in the center of a preheated oven at 375°F for 10–12 minutes. Remove the foil and beans, brush with the beaten egg yolk, and cook for a further 5 minutes until golden.

Remove the pie crust from the oven, let it cool slightly, then pour the filling into the crust and bake at the same temperature for 25–30 minutes until risen and brown.

Remove from the oven and let cool in the pan for 10 minutes, then transfer to a wire rack to cool completely. Arrange the figs, cut side up, on top of the tart. Warm the raspberry jelly and lightly brush the figs with it.

Protect the edges of the pie crust with aluminum foil to prevent over-browning, then preheat the broiler and set the tart close to the heat. Broil quickly until the figs are just browning, then serve immediately.

This amazingly popular dessert is said to have originated in Venice in the 1950s, and is one that actually benefits from being made the day before. For added texture, I like to grind real chocolate in a blender for layering and sprinkling. Some recipes are too sweet for my taste, but you can add more sugar to the cream mixture if you like. Make this in a large glass dish or in individual glasses for a special occasion.

tiramisù con lampone

6 oz. bittersweet chocolate

1¼ cups heavy cream

½ cup Italian espresso coffee

6 tablespoons Marsala wine

8 oz. mascarpone cheese (1 cup)

⅛ cup sugar

2 tablespoons dark rum

2 egg yolks

24 savoiardi or ladyfingers

1 pint fresh raspberries, plus extra to serve

a serving dish or 4 glasses

serves 4 generously

Put the chocolate in a blender or food processor and grind to a powder. Set aside. Pour the cream into a bowl and whisk until soft peaks form. Set aside.

Pour the espresso into a second bowl and stir in 2 tablespoons of the Marsala. Set aside. Put the mascarpone in a third bowl and whisk in 3 tablespoons of the sugar, then beat in 2 tablespoons of the Marsala and the rum. Set aside.

To make the zabaglione mixture, put the egg yolks, 2 tablespoons Marsala, and the remaining 2 tablespoons sugar in a medium heatproof bowl and beat with a hand-held electric mixer or whisk until well blended. Set over a saucepan of gently simmering water—the bottom should at no time be in contact with the water, and don't let the water boil. Whisk the mixture until it is glossy, pale, light, and fluffy and holds a trail when dropped from the whisk. This should take about 5 minutes. Remove from the heat and whisk until cold. Fold in the whipped cream, then fold in the mascarpone mixture.

Dip the savoiardi, one at a time, into the espresso mixture. Do not leave them in for too long or they will disintegrate. Start assembling the tiramisù by arranging half the dipped savoiardi in the bottom of a serving dish or 4 glasses. Trickle over some of the leftover espresso. Add a layer of raspberries.

Sprinkle with one-third of the ground chocolate, then add half the zabaglione-cream-mascarpone mixture. Arrange the remaining savoiardi on top, moisten with any remaining espresso, add some more raspberries and sprinkle with half the remaining chocolate. Finally spoon over the remaining zabaglione-cream-mascarpone and finish with a thick layer of chocolate and extra raspberries. Chill in the refrigerator for at least 3 hours (overnight is better) for the flavors to develop. Serve chilled.

This is the Italian version of English trifle and is found in many variations, often containing chopped candied fruit. It is probably called "English soup" because the sponge layer at the bottom acts like the bread base of a traditional Italian *zuppa*, absorbing the custard. In the south of Italy, it is topped with meringue and becomes almost a French *îles flottante* with cake. In Tuscany, it is served very liquid and soupy. My version has the meringue topping that I find makes the whole thing lighter. The traditional liqueur to use is a shocking pink, so you can add a little pink food coloring to any liqueur you are using to give the same effect.

zuppa inglese

10 oz. plain sponge cake

1 cup rum

½ cup Alchermes (pink Italian liqueur), Rosolio, Aurum, or any orange-flavored liqueur such as Cointreau

pink coloring (optional)

vanilla custard

3⅔ cups whole milk

1 vanilla bean, split

8 eggs, separated (4 whites reserved)

½ cup plus 1 tablespoon sugar, plus extra for sprinkling

2 tablespoons all-purpose flour

a deep heatproof ceramic or glass dish

serves 6

Slice the cake thinly, cutting off any brown edges. Mix the rum and liqueur in a measuring cup and add coloring, if using. Line the base of the dish with one-third of the sliced cake. Sprinkle with ½ cup of the rum mixture.

Make the custard now because it has to be warm when layering so it can soak into the cake.

Put the milk and vanilla bean in a saucepan and heat to just under boiling point. Put the egg yolks and 5½ tablespoons of the sugar in a bowl and beat until pale and fluffy. Beat in the flour. Gradually whisk in the hot milk. Return the saucepan to the stove and cook over low heat, stirring constantly with a wooden spoon for about 10 minutes or until thickened to a pourable custard consistency. Remove the vanilla bean, rinse and dry, and keep in the sugar jar.

Pour one-third of the custard over the cake and let it soak in for 5 minutes. Repeat with the second third of cake and another 100 ml of the rum mixture, pouring in half the remaining custard. Repeat once more using up all the cake, rum mixture, and custard. Let cool completely—the custard will develop a skin, but don't worry. Chill for 2–3 hours.

To finish, whisk the 4 egg whites in a bowl with the remaining sugar until thick and glossy and holding soft peaks. Spoon this carefully over the *zuppa* in blobs, then join the blobs together and use the back of a spoon to make swirls in the meringue. Sprinkle with extra sugar and heat under a medium broiler for 1 minute until lightly colored. Serve while the meringue is still warm. It can be chilled again, but the meringue won't look so spectacular.

Gianduja or *gianduia* is a chocolate and hazelnut mixture, famously associated with Turin, and is often used to flavor ice cream. This version of ice cream is classed as a *semifreddo*, which means that it remains soft when frozen, because of the meringue base.

profiteroles con sorpresa

gianduja semifreddo

1 cup blanched, toasted hazelnuts

4 oz. bittersweet chocolate, broken up

2¾ cups heavy cream

2 eggs, separated

¾ cup plus 2 tablespoons confectioners' sugar

choux pastry dough

6 tablespoons unsalted butter, cubed

⅔ cup all-purpose flour, sifted twice with a pinch of salt

2–3 large eggs, beaten

hot chocolate sauce

4 oz. bittersweet chocolate

1 cup heavy cream

3 tablespoons sugar

3 tablespoons butter

a freezer container, 5 cup capacity

3 baking sheets, lined with nonstick parchment paper

serves 6

To make the semifreddo, grind the hazelnuts very finely. Put the chocolate in a heatproof bowl over a saucepan of hot water and let melt.

Put the cream in a bowl and whisk until soft peaks form, then fold in the nuts. Put the egg yolks in a second bowl with 2 tablespoons of the sugar and whisk until pale and creamy. Put the egg whites in a clean dry bowl and whisk until soft peaks form. Add the remaining sugar to the whites, spoonful by spoonful, whisking between each addition, until very thick.

Stir the chocolate into the egg yolk mixture. Fold in the cream, then the meringue mixture. Spoon into a freezer container and freeze for 12 hours until firm. Put a lined baking sheet in the freezer. Take the ice cream out of the freezer and put it in the refrigerator for 10 minutes before scooping into small balls with an ice cream scoop and setting apart on the frozen baking sheet. Freeze until hard.

To make the choux pastry for the profiteroles, put the butter and 1 cup plus 2 tablespoons water in a heavy saucepan and bring slowly to a boil, so that by the time the water boils, the butter is completely melted. As soon as it hits a rolling boil, add all the flour all at once, remove the pan from the heat, and beat well with a wooden spoon. It is ready when the mixture leaves the sides of the pan.

Let cool slightly, then beat in the eggs, a little at a time, until the mixture is very smooth and shiny. If the eggs are large, it may not be necessary to add all of them. The mixture should just flop off the spoon when you bang it on the side of the pan—it should not be runny. Set teaspoons of the mixture at least 3 inches apart on a lined baking sheet and bake in a preheated oven at 400°F for 20–30 minutes or until deep golden brown.

Remove from the oven and split each one almost in two. Return to the oven to dry out for about 5 minutes. Cool on a wire rack. To assemble, put an ice cream ball in each one, pushing the halves almost together. Store in a box in the freezer until needed. Pile into a dish and soften in the refrigerator for 10 minutes before serving.

To make the hot chocolate sauce, put the chocolate, cream, sugar, and butter in a saucepan. Stir until melted and pour immediately over the profiteroles.

Fluffy little puffs like this are very popular, and are found in many guises. There is usually one to suit each saint, for his or her particular Saint's Day. Deep-fried snacks like these are part of Italian life and are seen as a real festive treat.

fluffy ricotta fritters

frittelle di ricotta

1 cup ricotta cheese

2 eggs, at room temperature

2 tablespoons sugar

1 teaspoon pure vanilla extract

¾ cup all-purpose flour

1 teaspoon baking powder

½ teaspoon salt

vegetable oil, for frying

confectioners' sugar, to serve

an electric deep-fryer

a tray lined with paper towels

serves 4–6

Press the ricotta through a food mill, potato ricer, or sieve into a large bowl. Put the eggs, sugar, and vanilla in a second bowl and whisk until pale and light. Fold into the ricotta.

Sift the flour with the baking powder and salt into a bowl, then fold it into the cheese and egg mixture.

Heat the vegetable oil in the deep-fryer to 375°F. Have a tray lined with paper towels and a slotted spoon or strainer at the ready.

Drop level tablespoons of the mixture into the hot oil in batches of 6. Fry for 2–3 minutes until puffed and deep brown all over (you may have to turn them in the oil). Drain and serve immediately, dusted with confectioners' sugar.

negroni

1 oz. gin

1 oz. Campari

¾ oz. sweet (red) vermouth

a wide twist of unwaxed orange zest

a cocktail shaker

serves 1

Though an aperitivo, not a digestivo, this is the best cocktail, in or out of Italy. It was invented by a Florentine nobleman, Camillo Negroni. He added a drop of gin to his favorite cocktail, the Americano (Campari, red vermouth and soda), for extra kick.

Put the gin, Campari, and vermouth in an ice-filled cocktail shaker. Shake until well chilled and strain into a chilled cocktail glass.

Cut a piece of orange zest about 1 x 2 inches. There must be no white pith attached—this will stop the oil being released from the zest. Holding the orange zest in one hand, hold a lit match over the glass with the other. Hold the orange zest about 1 inch above the flame, and squeeze the zest quickly. When done correctly, a burst of flame will come from the oils being released from the orange zest, leaving their aroma and adding a note of burnt orange to the cocktail. Drop the twist into the drink and serve immediately.

limoncello

2 large unwaxed lemons, plus the freshly squeezed juice of 1 lemon

2 cups clear liquor, such as vodka or grappa

1¾ cups sugar

a preserving jar, at least 1 pint

sterilized bottles, 3 cups total

makes about 3 cups

Delicious and wickedly refreshing. Many trattorias make their own—and when it runs out, you have to wait a long time for the new batch. It is best kept in the freezer and poured into frozen glasses. It is made wherever lemons are grown, especially the Amalfi coast.

Wash and scrub the lemons in warm soapy water. Rinse and dry. Carefully peel the zest from the lemons in long strips and put in a large preserving jar. Pour over the liquor, seal tightly, and leave in a dark place for 2 months.

After 2 months, put the sugar in a saucepan with 1 cup water and the strained juice of 1 lemon. Heat gently until the sugar dissolves. Cool. Open the preserving jar with the lemon-flavored liquor, and pour in the sugar syrup. Stir well, and let stand for 2–3 hours. Strain through a fine sieve or coffee paper and pour into sterilized bottles. Seal and leave in a cool dark place for 1 week. Store in the freezer, where it will thicken but not freeze.

basics

fresh egg pasta

pasta all'uovo

Nothing beats homemade pasta—not even store-bought "fresh." The texture is silky and the cooked dough itself very light. These quantities are only guidelines—depending on humidity, type of flour used, and other factors, you may have to add more or less flour. I like to use a mixture of 50 percent Italian-style flour and 50 percent *farina di semola* (finely ground hard wheat flour for making pasta and some breads). This mixture of soft and hard wheat flours gives the dough a certain "bite." The dough must not be too soft—it should require some effort when kneading! However, too much extra flour will make the pasta too tough to handle and, when cooked, taste floury. Generally allow one egg to 100 g flour per portion for an entrée.

1⅓ cups all-purpose flour (or use "Italian-style" flour—see recipe introduction)

a pinch of salt

2 large eggs

1 tablespoon olive oil, plus extra (see method)

a pasta machine or rolling pin

serves 2–4

Sift the flour and salt onto a clean work surface and make a hollow in the center with your fist.

Put the eggs and oil in a bowl, beat well, then pour into the hollow in the flour. Gradually mix the eggs into the flour with the fingers of one hand, and bring it together to form a dough.

Knead the pasta until smooth, lightly massage with a hint of olive oil, put in a plastic bag, and let rest for at least 30 minutes before attempting to roll out. The pasta will be much more elastic after resting. Roll out by hand or machine.

Feed the rested dough several times through the widest setting first, folding in 3 each time. Then roll the pasta through all the settings, reducing the settings until reaching the required thickness. Generally the second from last setting is best for tagliatelle, the finest being for ravioli or pasta that is to be filled.

After the required thickness is reached, hang the pasta over a broom handle to dry a little–this will make cutting it easier in humid weather, because it will not be so sticky. However, ravioli should be made immediately, because it should be slightly sticky to adhere properly.

Pass the pasta through the chosen cutters then drape the cut pasta over the broom handle again until ready to cook. Alternatively, toss the cut pasta lightly in flour (preferably semolina flour) and use as soon as possible, or transfer to a tray covered with a clean cloth sprinkled with a little flour.

Variations

Spinach Pasta *Pasta Verde*

1 cup frozen leaf spinach (cooked and squeezed of as much moisture as possible)

Pasta all'Uovo ingredients as for the previous recipe, but use 1 extra large egg instead of 2 large

a pinch of salt and freshly ground black pepper

Cook the spinach according to the package instructions, drain, then squeeze out as much moisture as possible.

Sift the flour onto a clean work surface and make a hollow in the middle. Put the spinach, egg, salt, and pepper in a blender and blend until smooth. Pour into the hollow in the flour and proceed as in the first recipe above.

Tomato Pasta

Pasta all'Uovo ingredients as for the first recipe, but use 1 extra-large egg instead of 2 large

2 tablespoons tomato purée or sun-dried tomato paste

Add the tomato purée or sun-dried tomato paste to the hollow in the flour and proceed as in the basic recipe on page 137.

Beet Pasta

Pasta all'Uovo ingredients as for the first recipe, but use 1 extra-large egg instead of 2 large

2 tablespoons grated cooked beet

Put the grated cooked beet, eggs, salt, and pepper in a blender and blend until smooth. Pour into the hollow in the flour and proceed as in the first recipe on page 137.

Saffron Pasta

1 sachet powdered saffron

Pasta all'Uovo ingredients as for the first recipe, but use 1 extra-large egg instead of 2 large

Soak the powdered saffron in 2 tablespoons hot water for 15 minutes. Beat the egg, then whisk in the saffron water before adding to the flour. Proceed as in the first recipe on page 137.

Herb Pasta

Pasta all'Uovo ingredients as for the first recipe

3 tablespoons finely chopped fresh herbs

Add the herbs to the flour and proceed as in the first recipe on page 137.

Black Pasta

Pasta all'Uovo ingredients as for the first recipe

1 sachet of squid ink

Beat the squid ink into the eggs before adding to the flour. A little extra flour may be needed. Proceed as in the first recipe on page 137.

cooking pasta

Put the pasta in a large saucepan of boiling salted water (as a guide, use 4 quarts water and 2–3 tablespoons salt for every 13–16 oz. fresh or dried pasta).

Stir once or twice to prevent sticking. If you have enough water in the pan and you stir the pasta as it goes in, it shouldn't stick. DO NOT COVER, or the water will boil over. Quickly bring the pasta back to a rolling boil, stir, and boil until *al dente* or "to the bite/tooth," which means that the pasta should be just firm to the bite. It should not have a hard center or be very floppy. Calculate the cooking time from the moment the pasta starts to boil again. Have a colander ready in the sink.

Quickly drain the pasta, reserving 2–3 tablespoons of the cooking water, returning the pasta to the pan with the reserved water. This will help the sauce to cling to the pasta. Dress the pasta immediately with the sauce, oil, or butter directly in the pan. Serve hot pasta straight away.

The Italian way is to toss the pasta with the sauce before serving.

Note: Fresh unfilled pasta takes 1–3 minutes (some very thin pasta is ready as soon as the water returns to a boil).

Dried unfilled pasta takes about 8–12 minutes, but keep checking as this is only a rough guide.

Fresh filled pasta takes 8–10 minutes to cook and dried filled pasta will take 15–20 minutes.

béchamel sauce

besciamella

This creamy sauce is the basis of many comforting pasta dishes, and equally good with meat, vegetable, and fish dishes. The secret to *besciamella* is to use more butter than flour and cook the flour in the butter for at least 5 minutes before adding the milk. Everyone has their own way of preventing lumps. I take the pan off the heat and add the cold milk all at once, whisking furiously before returning it to the heat to thicken and cook. A fresh bay leaf or freshly grated nutmeg are good additions.

6 tablespoons butter

⅓ cup all-purpose flour

about 2 cups milk

sea salt

makes 2 cups sauce

Melt the butter in a medium saucepan. When foaming, add the flour and cook over gentle heat for about 5 minutes without letting it brown. Have a balloon whisk ready. Slide off the heat and add all the milk at once, whisking very well. When all the flour and butter have been amalgamated and there are no lumps, return to the heat and slowly bring to a boil, whisking all the time. When it comes to a boil, add salt, simmer gently for 2–3 minutes, then use immediately.

If making in advance, cover the surface directly with plastic wrap to prevent a skin forming, then let cool. When reheating, remove the plastic and reheat very gently, stirring every now and then until liquid. (You may need to whisk it to remove lumps.) If using for lasagne, don't worry too much about lumps—they will disappear when the whole dish cooks. If you like a thinner sauce, just add extra milk after it has boiled and thickened.

the pizza maker's tomato sauce

salsa pizzaiola

Pizzaiola sauce is named after the traditional sauce that a pizza maker would put on the base of a pizza. It is a speciality of Naples, but common throughout Italy. To acquire its distinctive, concentrated, almost caramelized flavor, the tomatoes must cook at a very lively heat in a shallow pan. This sauce has a hundred different uses and is particularly delicious served with steaks and grilled or broiled fish.

½ cup olive oil

2 garlic cloves, chopped

1 teaspoon dried (not fresh) oregano

1¾ lb. fresh tomatoes, peeled and coarsely chopped or 28 oz. canned chopped tomatoes

sea salt and freshly ground black pepper

serves 4

Put the oil in a large, shallow pan and heat almost to smoking point (a wok is good for this). Standing back (it will splutter if it's at the right temperature), add the garlic, oregano, and tomatoes.

Cook over a fierce heat for 5–8 minutes or until the sauce is thick and glossy. Season with salt and pepper.

classic pesto

When made with the freshest of ingredients, this sauce from Liguria is a brilliant green—the color of lush new grass. Pesto freezes well, so when the best basil is around in the summer, I freeze it in ice-cube trays, then transfer the cubes into plastic bags. Don't thaw the cubes, just let them melt into whatever's cooking. This is the most wonderful sauce in the world.

2 garlic cloves, peeled

½ cup pine nuts

2 oz. fresh basil leaves without stalks (about 1½ cups)

⅔ cup good olive oil

4 tablespoons unsalted butter, softened

¼ cup freshly grated Parmesan or aged pecorino cheese

sea salt and freshly ground black pepper

serves 4

Classic method Using a mortar and pestle, pound the garlic and pine nuts with a little salt until broken. Add the basil leaves, a few at a time, pounding and mixing to a paste. Gradually beat in the olive oil, little by little, until the mixture is creamy and thick. Beat in the butter and season with pepper, then beat in the cheese. Spoon into a jar with a layer of olive oil on top to exclude the air, store in the refrigerator until needed, making sure you level the surface each time you use it, and re-cover with olive oil.

For those without much time or a mortar and pestle
Put everything in a blender or food processor and process until the pesto is as smooth as you like.

red pesto

Long before red pesto appeared in jars, I made this punchy, robust sauce to remind me of southern Italy. The chile is essential, giving a special kick. Don't be tempted to skimp on the basil—it is important for the right balance of flavor. Only wash the leaves if you have to—many Italians grow their own, even if they just have a balcony, and homegrown basil will usually be pesticide-free. By washing it, you remove essential oils and the basil can go soggy and start to turn black. If you do wash the leaves, use paper towels to pat thoroughly dry.

1 large red pepper

2 oz. fresh basil leaves without stalks (about 1½ cups)

1 garlic clove, crushed

2 tablespoons pine nuts, toasted

2 very ripe tomatoes

6 sun-dried tomatoes in oil, drained

3 tablespoons tomato paste

½ teaspoon mild chile powder

½ cup freshly grated Parmesan or aged pecorino cheese

⅔ cup extra virgin olive oil

serves 4

Grill the whole pepper, turning until blackened all over. Peel off the skin under running water, cut in half, and remove the stalk and seeds.

Put in a food processor with the basil, garlic, pine nuts, tomatoes, sun-dried tomatoes, tomato paste, chile powder, and Parmesan and blend until smooth. With the machine running, slowly pour in the olive oil. Spoon into a jar and cover with a layer of olive oil. Will keep in the refrigerator for up to 2 weeks, topped up with olive oil as you use it.

websites and mail order

Bartolini
Via dei Servi 30/r,
Santissima Annunziata, Florence, Italy
Italian cookware shop—temple of gastronomy.

Baroni
Mercato Centrale, Florence, Italy
www.baronialimentari.it
*The Baroni family offers top-quality condiments,
oils, aged balsamic vinagars, fresh alpine butter,
fresh black and white truffles in season, and truffle
products and will ship all over the world. Visit
when next in Florence, or visit the site to be
transported.*

www.chefshop.com
877-337-2491
P.O. Box 3488,
Seattle, WA 98114
*Features a wide range of quality raw ingredients,
plus condiments and seasonings.*

www.esperya.com
*Genuine, high quality foods from all regions of
Italy (olive oil, wine, honey, pasta, rice, desserts,
charcuterie, cheeses, preserves, seafood).*

www.gamberorosso.it
*Fascinating Italian gastronomic website (English
version under construction)—books, food, wine.*

www.italianmade.com
The Italian Trade Commission,
33 E 67th Street, New York, NY 10021
*The US official site of the foods and wines of Italy.
Includes how to eat Italian-style, where to eat and
buy Italian produce in the US, history, and lore of
Italian foods and wines.*

www.italianwinereview.com
*Interesting and impartial news and information
about Italian wines.*

www.kingarthurflour.com
800-827-6836
P.O. Box 876,
Norwich, VT 05055
*King Arthur Flour, Vermont's venerable milling
company, has on-line site and catalog called "The
Bakers Catalogue" that is an invaluable resource
for serious (and not-so-serious) bread bakers. You
may order every flour imaginable including, Italian-
style, spelt, buckwheat, triticale flours, plus malt
products and other baking aids. Knowledgeable
staff members are available to answer baking
questions: call 802-649-3717.*

www.menu2menu.com/italglossary.html
*Helpful glossary of Italian menu and cooking
terms.*

www.penzeys.com
800-741-7787
*Penzeys Spice offers more than 250 herbs,
spices, and seasonings, including blue
poppyseeds, white, green, or pink peppercorns,
white and green cardamom, and premium saffron.
Shop on-line, request a catalog, or explore any
one of 16 Penzeys Spice shops nationwide.*

www.zingermans.com
620 Phoenix Drive,
Ann Arbor, Michigan 48108
888-636-8162 or 734-663-DELI
422 Detroit Street
Ann Arbor, Michigan 48104
*What began in 1982 as small deli with great
sandwiches has grown to a global foods paradise.
Zingerman's selection of cheeses, estate-bottled
olive oils, and varietal vinegars is unmatched. Their
website and catalog are packed with information.*

index

conversion charts

Weights and measures have been rounded up
or down slightly to make measuring easier.

Volume equivalents:

American	Metric	Imperial
1 teaspoon	5 ml	
1 tablespoon	15 ml	
¼ cup	60 ml	2 fl.oz.
⅓ cup	75 ml	2½ fl.oz.
½ cup	125 ml	4 fl.oz.
⅔ cup	150 ml	5 fl.oz. (¼ pint)
¾ cup	175 ml	6 fl.oz.
1 cup	250 ml	8 fl.oz.

Weight equivalents:

Imperial	Metric
1 oz.	25 g
2 oz.	50 g
3 oz.	75 g
4 oz.	125 g
5 oz.	150 g
6 oz.	175 g
7 oz.	200 g
8 oz. (½ lb.)	250 g
9 oz.	275 g
10 oz.	300 g
11 oz.	325 g
12 oz.	375 g
13 oz.	400 g
14 oz.	425 g
15 oz.	475 g
16 oz. (1 lb.)	500 g
2 lb.	1 kg

Measurements:

Inches	cm
¼ inch	5 mm
½ inch	1 cm
¾ inch	1.5 cm
1 inch	2.5 cm
2 inches	5 cm
3 inches	7 cm
4 inches	10 cm
5 inches	12 cm
6 inches	15 cm
7 inches	18 cm
8 inches	20 cm
9 inches	23 cm
10 inches	25 cm
11 inches	28 cm
12 inches	30 cm

Oven temperatures:

110°C	(225°F)	Gas ¼
120°C	(250°F)	Gas ½
140°C	(275°F)	Gas 1
150°C	(300°F)	Gas 2
160°C	(325°F)	Gas 3
180°C	(350°F)	Gas 4
190°C	(375°F)	Gas 5
200°C	(400°F)	Gas 6
220°C	(425°F)	Gas 7
230°C	(450°F)	Gas 8
240°C	(475°F)	Gas 9